2019 / 2020

EVENTDESIGN JAHRBUCH
EVENT DESIGN YEARBOOK

2019 / 2020

EVENTDESIGN JAHRBUCH
EVENT DESIGN YEARBOOK

Katharina Stein

avedition

INHALT
CONTENTS

Was lange Zeit gefordert wurde, ist nun in der breiten Praxis der Live-Kommunikation angekommen. Der Mensch und seine Interessen werden stärker berücksichtigt – in der inhaltlichen Konzeption, in Möglichkeiten zur Teilnahme und Teilhabe und in zeitlichen sowie räumlichen Wahlfreiheiten.

Vorbei scheinen die Zeiten, in denen Marken ihre Produkte zentrieren und in eher starren, sich selbst feiernden Formaten zur Schau stellten. Nun fragt man sich, was die Besucher interessiert und begeistert. Nun möchte man sie entscheiden lassen, was sie wann, wo und wie erleben möchten.

Unter dem Druck des breiten Erlebnisangebots und verbunden mit dem Bestreben, ein Social-Media-Thema zu werden, rückt das eigene Produkt ein Stück in den Hintergrund, das Image wird wichtiger.

DIE MARKE WIRD ZUM FREUNDSCHAFT-LICHEN GASTGEBER, DAS PRODUKT ZUM SPIELERISCHEN, INTERAKTIVEN UND FOTOTAUGLICHEN ERLEBNIS.

Diese Entwicklung zeigt sich unter anderem in diversen Festival- und Convention-Formaten. Ein- oder mehrtägige Events, die künstlerische, informative und unterhaltende Programmpunkte miteinander verbinden und möglichst viele verschiedene Erlebnisarten anbieten. Die Begeisterung der Besucher für Themen, Handlungen oder Marken steht im Mittelpunkt – ebenso wie die möglichst effektive Anregung, diese in den sozialen Netzwerken kundzutun. Auch die zeitliche und räumliche Wahlfreiheit eines individuellen Programm- und Tagesablaufs spielt dabei eine große Rolle.

Darüber hinaus gehören Apps und Plattformen, die den Gästen die Möglichkeit bieten, sich einzubringen, an der Themengestaltung mitzuwirken oder mit anderen Teilnehmern in Kontakt zu kommen, zum guten Ton – vornehmlich bei Mitarbeiterevents.

Doch was so einfach klingt, kann eine Herausforderung sein. Auch wenn sich viele Menschen mehr Teilhabe wünschen – sie zur Teilnahme zu bewegen ist nicht immer leicht. Nur weil man eine App anbietet, bedeutet das nicht, dass sie auch genutzt wird. Wie also bringt man Menschen dazu, Interaktionsmöglichkeiten wahrzunehmen? Was sind die Stellschrauben für eine glaubwürdige Interaktion? Antworten liefern vier Fachfrauen und -männer im Interview ab Seite 8.

Andererseits fällt aber auch auf, wie ähnlich sich viele Konzepte sind. Man achte nur mal auf die äußerst beliebte Analogie der Stadt in diesem Buch. Da stellt sich unweigerlich die Frage, ob sich wirklich etwas geändert hat. Wird vorab tatsächlich mehr und individuell analysiert? Auch dazu gibt das Interview (S. 8) aufschlussreiche sowie entlarvende Antworten.

Abschließend möchte ich auf eine in diesem Jahr ganz neue Kategorie im Eventdesign Jahrbuch aufmerksam machen. Dank einer überraschenden Anzahl von eingereichten Studierendenprojekten präsentiert die Kategorie „Student Projects" kategorieübergreifende Arbeiten verschiedener Hochschulteams. Der vielen Kritik am Eventnachwuchs zum Trotz beweisen manche dieser Projekte, dass sie locker mit professionellen Agenturen mithalten können.

Und nun viel Spaß beim Blättern und Diskutieren.

Katharina Stein

„DU ENTSCHEIDEST!" DER MENSCH IM FOKUS
"YOU DECIDE!" A FOCUS ON PEOPLE
INTRODUCTION BY KATHARINA STEIN

What was demanded for a long time has now established itself in the wider practice of live communication. People and their interests are taken into consideration to a greater extent – in the content concept, the possibilities for participation and involvement, as well as freedom of choice in terms of time and space.

It appears that the times in which brands placed their products at the centre and displayed them in rather rigid, self-celebratory formats are over. Now the question is what interests and enthuses visitors. Now the decision on what to experience when, where and how is left up to them.

Under the pressure of the wide range of experiences on offer and in connection with the endeavour to become a social media topic, the product itself is shifted a little more into the background and image is becoming more important.

THE BRAND IS BECOMING A FRIENDLY HOST, THE PRODUCT IS BECOMING A PLAYFUL, INTER-ACTIVE AND PHOTO-GENIC EXPERIENCE.

This development is evident, for example, in various festival and convention formats. Single-day or multiple-day events that combine artistic, informative and entertaining programme elements and offer as many different types of experience as possible. The enthusiasm of the visitors for topics, activities or brands is the focus – as well as the most effective encouragement to broadcast these on social media networks. The freedom of choice in terms of time and space regarding an individual programme and schedule play an important role in this.

In addition, apps and platforms that allow guests to contribute, participate in the topics or establish contact with other participants are all part of it – especially for employee events.

However, what sounds so simple can be a challenge. Even if many people wish for greater involvement – it is not always easy to prompt them to participate. Just because one offers an app does not mean that it will also be used. How does one therefore get people to make use of interaction possibilities? What are the drivers of credible interaction? Four specialist women and men provide answers in the interview starting on page 8.

On the other hand, it is also noticeable how similar many concepts are. One only needs to note the exceptionally popular analogy of the city in this book. This undoubtedly raises the question of whether anything has really changed. Is there really greater individual analysis in advance? The interview (p. 8) also provides insightful and revealing answers to this.

To conclude, I would like to draw attention to a whole new category in the Event Design Yearbook this year. Owing to the surprising number of student projects that were submitted, the category "Student Projects" presents the work of various university teams across different categories. Despite the wealth of criticism directed at up-and-coming event designers, some of these projects prove that they can easily stand their ground against professional agencies.

And now we wish you enjoyable browsing and discussions.

Katharina Stein

Im diesjährigen Eventdesign Jahrbuch fällt auf, dass viele Veranstaltungen ihre Gäste deutlich stärker einbeziehen, als es noch vor wenigen Jahren der Fall war. Sowohl die inhaltliche Gestaltung, interaktive Teilnahme- und Teilhabemöglichkeiten als auch individuelle Wahlmöglichkeiten und räumliche Freiheiten haben sich im Sinne der Besucher gewandelt.

Woher kommt diese Entwicklung?

Stephan Müller:

Ich denke, einen großen Anteil an dieser Entwicklung hat die zunehmende Messbarkeit der Besuchererlebnisse. Vor ein paar Jahren basierte die Auswertung von Live-Kommunikation auf der Besucherzahl. Daran lässt sich aber nicht ablesen, ob den Besuchern die Ausstellung oder die Messe gefallen hat.

Mittlerweile bekommen Kunde und Agentur Feedback in den sozialen Netzwerken. Damit meine ich vor allem Posts bei Instagram, Facebook, Twitter oder YouTube.

Gehören Interaktionsmöglichkeiten und Co-Creation zu einem zeitgemäßen Event?

Stephan Schäfer-Mehdi:

Es ist eine Frage der Erwartungshaltung und der Kommunikationsaufgabe. Menschen gehen ja nach wie vor ins Theater und Kino und lassen sich von Kunst und Künstlern begeistern, ohne dass es vorher Co-Creation gab. Es gibt sicher immer noch Live-Kommunikation, die eher einen Informationscharakter hat und gerade große Menschenmengen ansprechen und begeistern muss, da ist die Einbeziehung der Besucher marginal möglich.

Bei anderen, kleineren Formaten ist die Einbeziehung der Besucher und Besucherinnen besser möglich. Eigentlich müsste man bei der Konzeption schon mit Co-Creation arbeiten. Aber angesichts der Preisdrückerei sehe ich im Augenblick nicht die Ressourcen für solche sinnvollen Prozesse.

Haben sich konzeptionelle Vorgehensweisen in diesem Kontext verändert?

Tomke Hahn:

Menschen wollen aus ihrem Alltag entführt werden. Die räumliche Gestaltung hilft, sie in einen anderen Zustand zu versetzen und für die Vermittlung von Inhalten zu öffnen. Das war immer schon so, aber die Erwartungshaltung der Besucher hat sich verändert und das wirkt sich natürlich auf das Konzept aus. Das Zusammenspiel aus Lichtstimmung, Temperatur, Raumklang, Duft und der Position des Menschen im Raum – stehend, sitzend, liegend – muss neue Perspektiven eröffnen. Perspektiven, die der Besucher annimmt und für sich nutzen kann.

Dagmar Korintenberg:

Einige Bedürfnisse, die sich in den letzten Jahren entwickelt haben, sollten bei der Planung auf jeden Fall mitgedacht werden. Der Wunsch vieler Besucher, sich und den eigenen Alltag medial zu präsentieren, hat beispielsweise deutlich an Stellenwert zugenommen. Um eine Veranstaltung gerade auch für eine jüngere Zielgruppe interessant zu gestalten, sollten also Erlebnisse geschaffen werden, die visuell neuartige und fotogene Momente integrieren.

Stephan Müller:

ES WIRD MEHR FÜR DAS ERLEBEN DES MOMENTS, DEN SPIELERISCHEN SPASS ODER DIE EINZIGARTIGKEIT GESTALTET.

Teilweise wird vom „Instagram Moment" gesprochen. Damit ist vor allem eine visuelle Stärke des Moments gemeint. Um wahrgenommen zu werden, benötigt ein

„LOS, MACH MIT!"
"COME ON, JOIN IN!"
INTERVIEW WITH TOMKE HAHN (SIMPLE), DAGMAR KORINTENBERG (RAUMSERVICE), STEPHAN MÜLLER (GROSSE 8) + STEPHAN SCHÄFER-MEHDI (LIVECOM)

In this year's Event Design Yearbook, one cannot help but notice that many events involve their guests to a significantly greater extent than was the case just a few years ago. Content design and interactive participation and involvement possibilities, as well as individual choices and spatial freedoms, have shifted in favour of the visitors.

What has caused this development?

Stephan Müller:

I think that the increasing measurability of visitor experiences has a lot to do with this development. A couple of years ago, the evaluation of live communication was based on the number of visitors. However, this does not reveal whether the visitors liked the exhibition or the trade fair.

In the meantime, the customer and the agency receive feedback on social networks. With this I especially mean posts on Instagram, Facebook, Twitter or YouTube.

Are interaction possibilities and co-creation essential aspects of a contemporary event?

Stephan Schäfer-Mehdi:

It is a question of expectations and the purpose of the communication. After all, people continue to go to the theatre and cinema and are enthused by art and artists, without co-creation beforehand. There is no doubt still live communication that has an information character and must appeal to and enthuse wide masses of people, in which case it is possible to incorporate the visitors marginally.

In other smaller formats, the involvement of the visitors is easier to manage. In fact, one should already work with co-creation when putting together the concept. However, in view of prize squeezing, I cannot see the resources at the moment for such purposeful processes.

Have conceptual procedures changed in this context?

Tomke Hahn:

People want to be enticed out of everyday life. The spatial design helps to transport them into new surroundings and open their minds towards the conveying of content. This has always been the case, but the expectations of visitors have changed and of course this has an impact on the concept. The interplay of lighting atmosphere, temperature, sound, scent and the position of the visitor in space – standing, sitting, lying – has to open up new perspectives. Perspectives the visitor adopts and knows how to make use of.

Dagmar Korintenberg:

Some requirements that have developed in recent years should definitely be considered during the planning stage. The wish of many visitors to present themselves and their own daily lives on media, for example, has gained significant importance. To design an event that is interesting especially also for a younger target group, experiences should be created that visually integrate novel and photogenic moments.

Stephan Müller:

CREATION IS MORE IN THE INTEREST OF EXPERIENCING THE MOMENT, PLAYFUL FUN OR UNIQUENESS.

In some cases, there is talk of the "Instagram moment", which refers primarily to the visual power of the moment. To be taken notice of, a post also needs a visual attractor.

Post auch einen visuellen Attraktor. Selbst eine Toninstallation müsste einen großen visuellen Impact liefern, um in den Netzwerken wirksam gepostet zu werden. Oft werden dadurch natürlich auch Dinge umgesetzt, die für den Livemoment eigentlich nicht wichtig, für eine Verbreitung in den sozialen Netzwerken aber unerlässlich sind.

Wird tatsächlich mehr analysiert, was sich Besucher wünschen?

Stephan Schäfer-Mehdi:

„Wir wissen, was unsere Pappenheimer wünschen", das ist immer noch die Alltagseinstellung in vielen Führungsetagen und Eventabteilungen. Ich bin da immer skeptisch und habe dann zum Beispiel auch mal Interviews geführt und deren Ergebnisse in die Konzeption einfließen lassen. Gerade wenn es um Change-Prozesse geht, ist das hilfreich.

Viele Menschen wünschen sich, stärker einbezogen zu werden. Trotzdem ist es manchmal schwer, sie zur Teilnahme zu bewegen. Wie bringt man Menschen dazu, sich einzubringen?

Tomke Hahn:

Die App ist ein gutes Beispiel. Viele Auftraggeber träumen von AR mit BYOD. Aber für die Besucher ist das Runterladen der App einfach nur lästig. Wichtig ist es deshalb, die Rolle des Besuchers und die damit verknüpften Erwartungen klar zu formulieren. Die Kunst ist es, die Erwartungen dabei niederschwellig, die Möglichkeiten aber weit offen zu halten.

Daneben spielen die kognitiven und physischen Zugänge sowie die Spielregeln eine entscheidende Rolle. Menschen sind sehr unterschiedlich und brauchen Einstiegsangebote, die zu ihnen passen. Während dem einen eine einfache Landkarte genügt, braucht der andere eine detaillierte Wegbeschreibung. Multiple Zugänge sind hier eine Lösung. Wir orientieren uns dabei an gelernten Prinzipien. Je natürlicher Handlungs- und Interaktionsabläufe sind, desto wahrscheinlicher ist ein kurzweiliger Ablauf und viele kleine und große Erfolgserlebnisse. Klare Spielregeln helfen, das Mitmachen einfach zu gestalten.

Dagmar Korintenberg:

OFTMALS IST DER MEHRWERT ENTSCHEIDEND FÜR DIE INTERAKTION DER BESUCHER.

Wenn beispielsweise das Einbringen von Inhalten ohne relevante Rückkopplungen für den Einzelnen als Partizipation verkauft wird, ist dies nicht besonders attraktiv. Vielmehr muss dem Beteiligten etwas zurückgegeben werden: Ein besonderes Erlebnis, spannender Gesprächsstoff für den kommenden Tag im Büro oder die mediale Nutzung, neue Erkenntnisse oder Formen von Teilhabe und Gemeinschaftserlebnissen.

Ersterlebnisse und das Schaffen von innovativen Situationen sind wichtige Parameter. Diese helfen den Besuchern, sich aus ihren festen, häufig passiven Rollen zu lösen, in Kommunikation mit den anderen Beteiligten zu treten und sich gemeinsam aktiv einzubringen. Ausschlaggebend ist zudem, ob man über das Maß der Interaktion selbst entscheiden kann – dass von einem Klick oder Handgriff bis hin zu aktiver Teilhabe alles möglich ist. Räumlich spiegelt sich diese Freiheit oftmals in modularen Lösungen wider, die aber in jedem Stadium sowohl inszenatorische, räumliche als auch visuelle Qualitäten aufweisen sollten.

Stephan Müller:

Neugierde wecken ist einer der Schlüssel. Teilnahme darf nicht bedeuten, dass man sich mit komplizierten Interaktionsmechanismen beschäftigen muss. Man darf nie aus den Augen verlieren, wie lange sich ein Besucher im Allgemeinen an einem Exponat oder in einen Ausstellungsraum aufhält. Da sprechen wir oft von wenigen Minuten. Wenn Besucher die Interaktion „erlernen" sollen oder müssen, dann hilft eine sehr spielerische Systematik hinter der Interaktion. Sie darf keine Berührungsängste erzeugen. Ausprobieren muss Spaß machen. Da kommen vor allem analoge Interfaces, weg vom digitalen Interface, infrage. Gestensteuerung ist da fehl am Platz.

Even a sound installation must deliver a great visual impact to be posted effectively on the networks. Of course, this often leads to the realisation of things that are not really important for the live moment but are essential for broadcasting on social networks.

Is there indeed more analysis regarding what visitors want?

Stephan Schäfer-Mehdi:

"We know what our people want," is still the general attitude on many management levels and in event departments. I am always sceptical in this regard and have also, for example, carried out interviews and allowed the results to flow into the concept. This is especially helpful when it is about change processes.

Many people would like to be more involved. Even so, it is sometimes difficult to prompt them to participate. What makes people get involved?

Tomke Hahn:

The app is a good example. Many clients dream of AR with BYOD. But for visitors, downloading the app is just an annoyance. It is important, therefore, to formulate the role of the visitor and the associated expectations. The art is to keep the expectation threshold low whilst keeping the possibilities wide open.

The cognitive and physical contact points, as well as the rules of the game, play a decisive role alongside this. People are very different and need access points that suit them. While a simple map is enough for some, others need a detailed route description. Multiple manners of access are a solution here. We orientate ourselves towards proven principles. The more natural action and interaction procedures are, the more likely it is to unfold in an entertaining manner with many minor and major success stories. Clear rules of the game help to make participation easy.

Dagmar Korintenberg:

IN MANY CASES, THE ADDED VALUE IS DECISIVE FOR VISITOR INTERACTION.

If, for example, the contribution of content is sold as participation without relevant feedback for the individual, it is not particularly attractive. Instead something must be given back to those involved: a special experience, an exciting discussion topic for the forthcoming day at the office, or the use of media, new insights or forms of participation and shared experiences.

First experiences and the creation of innovative situations are important parameters. These help visitors to release themselves from the fixed, often passive roles, to enter into communication with other participants and to contribute together actively. It is also decisive whether one can decide oneself about the degree of interaction – that everything is possible from a click or gesture to active participation. Spatially, this freedom is often reflected in modular solutions, which should however display scenographical, spatial and visual qualities at each stage.

Stephan Müller:

Awakening curiosity is one of the keys. Participation may not mean that one must be preoccupied with complicated interaction mechanisms. One must never lose sight of the fact of how long a visitor spends at an exhibit or in an exhibition room in general. In many cases, we are talking of just a few minutes. If visitors have to "learn" interaction, the interaction can be supported by a very playful approach. It must not provoke inhibitions. Trying out must be fun. Especially analogue interfaces, away from the digital interface, are possibilities here. Controlling gestures are inappropriate.

Ich habe das Gefühl, dass die Besucher durch die tagtägliche Nutzung von Smartphones und Tablets ein rein digitales Interface immer weniger als Erlebnis wahrnehmen. Wenn der Raum aber plötzlich reaktiv ist, und der Besucher ohne spezielle Interaktion auf die Veränderung des Raumes oder des Exponates Einfluss nehmen kann, dann erzeugt man spielerische Neugier.

Ob Apps, interaktive Stationen oder Workshopformate – dies sind mögliche Werkzeuge, aber keine Konzepte. Was sind die wahren Stellschrauben, um ein Erlebnis interaktiver und zielgruppenorientierter zu gestalten?

Stephan Schäfer-Mehdi:

UNABHÄNGIG DAVON, OB DIE KOMMUNIKATION DIGITAL, ANALOG ODER MIT EINEM MIX ERFOLGT, AUTHENTIZITÄT UND RELEVANZ SIND WICHTIG.

Nur wenn die Besucher diese erkennen oder finden, werden sie echte Teil-Nehmer. Und es muss auch ein Ergebnis oder eine Veränderung durch die Teilnahme geben, sonst macht beim nächsten Mal niemand mehr mit.

Viele Unternehmen wollen ja auch keine unkontrollierte Interaktion. Da muss sich auf Führungsebene das Mindset ändern, damit sich Eventteilnehmer wie Mitarbeiter oder Partner auch wirklich im Vorfeld, beim Event und auch danach einbringen können. Da ist ein Kulturwandel gefordert, der natürlich durch digitale Möglichkeiten gefördert wird.

Ich glaube, es muss generell ein Paradigmenwandel stattfinden. Wir sehen Live-Kommunikation immer noch vom singulären, späteren Ergebnis oder der einzelnen Veranstaltung her. Dabei müssen wir viel stärker in langfristigen Prozessen und über einzelne Projekte hinaus denken.

Die Interviews führte Katharina Stein.

Tomke Hahn, concept and content at simple

Dagmar Korintenberg, owner of Raumservice

I have the feeling that, due to the daily use of smartphones and tablets, visitors pay less and less attention to a purely digital interface as an experience. However, if the surroundings are suddenly reactive and the visitor can have an influence on the changing of a space or the exhibit without special interaction, one generates a playful kind of curiosity.

Whether it is apps, interactive stations or workshop formats – these are possible tools but not concepts. What are the true cruxes for making an experience more interactive and target-group-orientated?

Stephan Schäfer-Mehdi:

INDEPENDENTLY OF WHETHER THE COMMUNICATION IS DIGITAL, ANALOGUE OR A MIX OF THE TWO, AUTHENTICITY AND RELEVANCE ARE IMPORTANT.

Only if visitors can recognise or find these do they become real participants "taking part". And there must also be a result or a change due to the participation, otherwise nobody will join in the next time.

After all, many companies do not want uncontrolled interaction. The mindset at management level needs to change here so that event participants such as employees or partners can truly be involved in advance, at the event and afterwards. A change in culture is required here, which is of course promoted by digital possibilities.

I think that there needs to be a paradigm shift in general. We still see live communication from the point of view of the singular later result or the individual event. Instead we must think much more in terms of long-term process and beyond individual projects.

The interviews were conducted by Katharina Stein.

Stephan Müller, Creative Lead at GROSSE 8

Stephan Schäfer-Mehdi, Creative + Strategic Hitchhiker and freelance Art Director LiveCom

Jede Zielgruppe hat unterschiedliche Bedürfnisse und Erwartungen. Dementsprechend sind Eventkonzepte im Idealfall nicht nur auf den Absender, sondern vor allem auf die Empfänger zugeschnitten.

PUBLIC: EINE BREITE ÖFFENT-LICHKEIT, DIE SICH AUS EINWOHNERN, TOURISTEN, PASSANTEN, FLANEUREN ETC. ZUFÄLLIG ZUSAMMENSETZT. DEMENTSPRECHEND HETEROGEN – IN (SOZIALER) HERKUNFT, ALTER ODER VORLIEBEN – ZEIGT SICH DIESE ZIELGRUPPE, DIE NICHT NUR SEHR GROSS, SONDERN IN DER ANSPRACHE NICHT EINDEUTIG ZU FASSEN IST. WAS DEN JEWEILIGEN PERSONEN ALLERDINGS GEMEIN IST, IST EIN NICHT KOMMERZIELLES INTERESSE.

Each target group has different requirements and expectations. Event concepts are therefore ideally not only geared towards the addressor, but especially towards the recipients.

PUBLIC: A WIDER PUBLIC IS COMPOSED BY CHANCE OF INHABITANTS, TOURISTS, PASSERS-BY ETC. THIS TARGET GROUP IS HETEROGENEOUS ACCORDINGLY – IN TERMS OF (SOCIAL) BACKGROUND, AGE OR PREFERENCES – AND IS NOT ONLY VERY LARGE, BUT ALSO DIFFICULT TO GRASP IN TERMS OF APPEAL. HOWEVER, WHAT THESE PEOPLE HAVE IN COMMON IS A NON-COMMERCIAL INTEREST.

MERCEDES PLATZ OPENING CEREMONY
FLORA&FAUNAVISIONS GMBH, BERLIN

Location
Mercedes Platz, Berlin

Client
AEG – Anschutz Entertainment Group

Month / Year
October 2018

Duration
1 day

Dramaturgy / Direction / Coordination / Graphics / Media
flora&faunavisions GmbH, Berlin

Lighting
Chris Moylan for flora&faunavisions GmbH

Pyrotechnics
Pyro-Passion Feuerwerke, Potsdam

Music
Jan Weigel for flora&faunavisions GmbH

Photos
flora&faunavisions GmbH, Berlin;
Thomas Saul, feuerwerk-fanpage.de

Entsprechend dem wachsenden Interesse vieler Marken, die Öffentlichkeit besser zu erreichen, transparenter und nahbarer zu wirken, steigt auch die Zahl öffentlicher Marketingevents. Man möchte den Menschen Unterhaltung, aber vor allem identitätsstiftende Ereignisse im Interesse der Unternehmen bieten. In diesem Kontext erhalten selbst neue Straßen oder Plätze aufwendige öffentliche Eröffnungsinszenierungen. Wie beispielsweise der Mercedes Platz und sein neu geschaffenes Vergnügungsviertel in Berlin-Friedrichshain.

In accordance with the growing interest of many brands in reaching the public better, more transparently and more approachably, the number of public marketing events is also increasing. One would like to offer the people entertainment, but especially identity-forging events in the interest of the companies. In this context, even new streets or squares receive elaborate public opening inaugurations. Such as Mercedes Platz and its newly created leisure quarter in Berlin-Friedrichshain.

DIE ERÖFFNUNG DES BERLINER MERCEDES PLATZ WIRD ZUM AUDIO-VISUELLEN ÖFFENTLICHEN SPEKTAKEL.

For the opening ceremony, flora&faunavisions was appointed to design an impressive audiovisual experience. The result was a 15-minute multimedia show that guided the visitors through a day in the life of the city and the newly opened Mercedes Platz. For this purpose, the agency used all architectural integrated media, as well as complementary lighting and video technology. A façade mapping, LED panels and towers, water fountains and live show elements were part of the public event. Fireworks formed the evening finale.

Für die Eröffnungszeremonie wurde flora&faunavisions beauftragt, ein beeindruckendes audiovisuelles Erlebnis zu entwerfen. Das Ergebnis war eine 15-minütige Multimediashow, die die Besucher durch einen Tag im Leben der Stadt und des neu eröffneten Mercedes Platz führte. Hierfür nutzte die Agentur alle architektonisch integrierten Medien sowie ergänzende Licht- und Videotechnik. Ein Fassadenmapping, LED-Panels und -Türme, Wasserfontänen und Live-Show-Elemente waren Teil des öffentlichen Ereignisses. Ein Feuerwerk bildete das abendliche Finale.

THE OPENING OF THE BERLIN MERCEDES PLATZ BECOMES AN AUDIOVISUAL PUBLIC SPECTACLE.

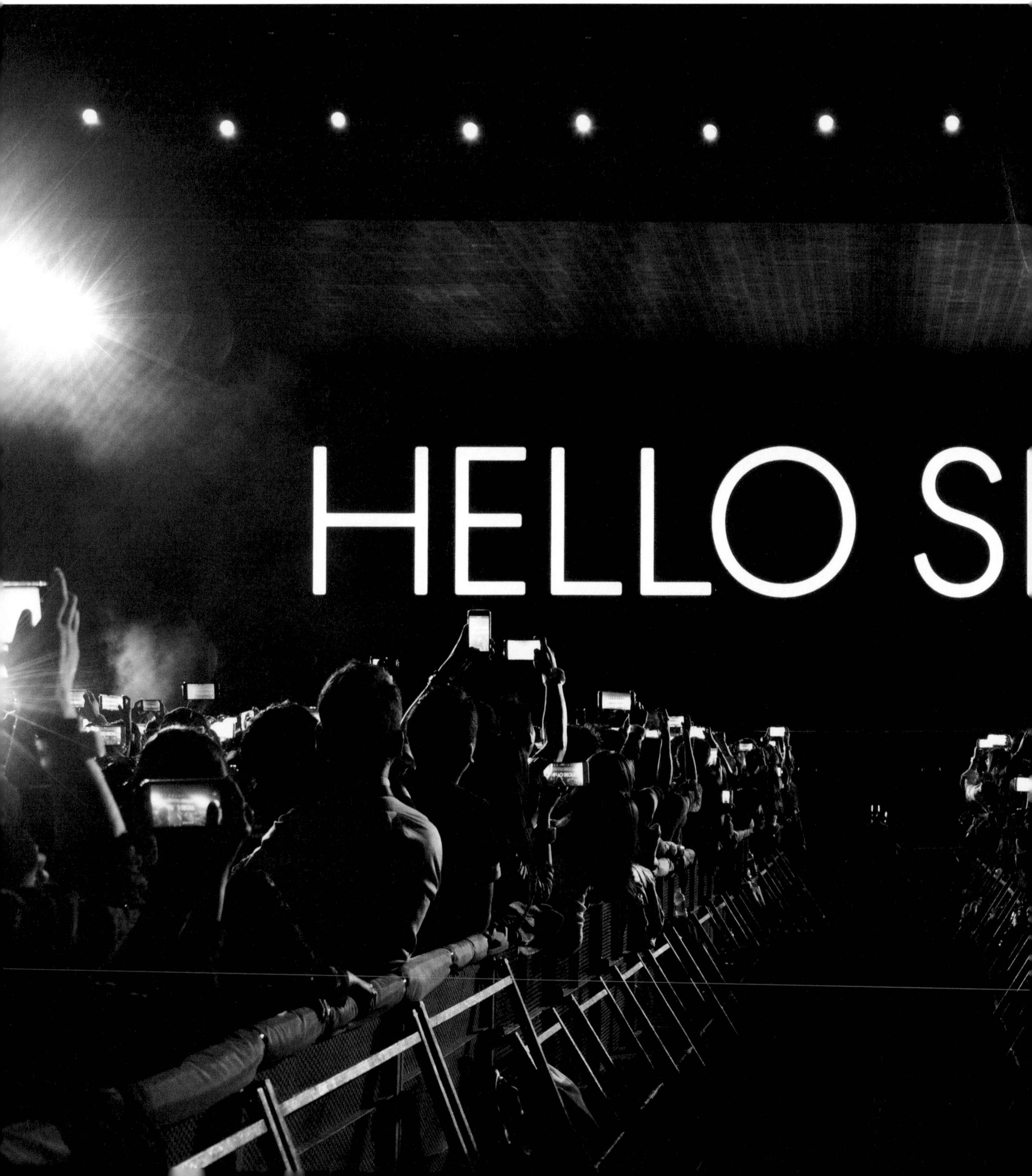
HELLO S

G70 FESTIVAL
BLACKSPACE, MUNICH

Location
Olympic Park, Seoul

Client
Genesis Motor Company, Seoul

Month / Year
September 2017

Duration
1 day

Awards
Silver from ADC Deutschland, Silver at CommAwards, Wood Pencil at D&AD Awards, DDC Award, Gold Medal at Golden Award Montreux, red dot communication design award

Dramaturgy
Anthony Randall

Direction / Coordination
TheBridgeCo; INNOCEAN Worldwide USA

Graphics
(CD) BLACKSPACE GmbH, Munich

Lighting
Martin Phillips

Media
Christian Lamb; TheBridgeCo

Film
BLACKSPACE GmbH, Munich

Music
Printz Board

Artists / Show acts
Gwen Stefani, Andra Day, Lee Chae-rin (CL), Printz Board

Realisation
Live Nation Korea

Photos
Christoph Hoidn (BLACKSPACE GmbH, Munich)

PRODUKTE UND MARKE RÜCKEN ZUGUNSTEN VON SYMBOLKRAFT UND GEMEINSAMEN MOMENTEN IN DEN HINTERGRUND.

Immer mehr Unternehmen und Marken erkennen, dass es nicht reicht, Produkte einfach nur aufwendig zu bewerben. Sie und die Marke müssen vielmehr zu einem Symbol werden. Marketingveranstaltungen müssen sich daher auf die Menschen, nicht die eigenen Produkte konzentrieren, sie müssen Zeichen setzen und ihre Besucher tatsächlich berühren. Einen solchen Ansatz hat die erste koreanische Luxus-Automarke Genesis zusammen mit BLACKSPACE verfolgt. In Zeiten, zu denen das geteilte Land immer wieder Thema weltpolitischer sowie lokaler Spannungen ist, wollte Genesis etwas bieten, worauf die Menschen stolz sein können – etwas, was sie zusammenführen soll.

More and more companies and brands are realising that it is not enough to simply advertise products at great expense. They and the brand must become more of a symbol. Marketing events must therefore focus on the people, not on their own products. They must set an example and actually touch their visitors. The first Korean luxury car brand Genesis pursued such an approach together with BLACKSPACE. In times in which the divided nation is often the subject of international political and local tension, Genesis wanted to offer something that the people could be proud of – something that would bring them together.

PRODUCTS AND BRAND BLEND INTO THE BACKGROUND IN FAVOUR OF POWERFUL SYMBOLS AND SHARED MOMENTS.

Gleichzeitig mit der Internationalen Automobil Ausstellung (IAA) 2017 in Frankfurt veranstaltete Genesis in diesem Sinne ein großes Festival. Jedoch Tausende Kilometer entfernt, in der Heimatstadt des Unternehmens Seoul. Die Vorstellung des neuen Wagenmodells G70 wurde zum Anlass genommen, 20.000 Freikarten für diese ungewöhnliche Großveranstaltung zu verschenken. Im Olympiapark der Stadt entwarf BLACKSPACE eine beeindruckende voll animierte Bühne und lud Stars wie Gwen Stefani, Andra Day und CL ein. Eine Modenschau von Jeremy Scott ergänzte das musikalische Angebot. In dieser Nacht wollte Genesis Motors nicht als Automobilunternehmen auftreten, sondern als Gastgeber eines Moments, der Menschen zusammenbringt und ein Zeichen setzt.

At the same time as the International Automobile Exhibition (IAA) 2017 in Frankfurt, Genesis held a corresponding big festival, but thousands of kilometers away in Seoul, the home city of the company. The introduction of the new car model G70 was taken as an occasion to give away 20.000 free tickets to this exceptional major event. BLACKSPACE designed an impressive, fully animated stage at the Olympic Park of the city and invited stars such as Gwen Stefani, Andra Day and CL. A fashion show by Jeremy Scott completed the musical contribution. During this night, Genesis Motors did not want to present themselves as an automobile enterprise but as the host of a moment that brings people together and points the way.

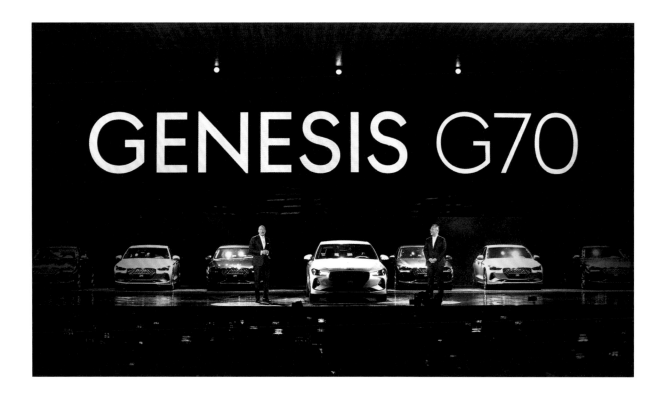

#WONACHSUCHSTDU – MAX PLANCK DAY SCIENCE AWARENESS CAMPAIGN
ONLIVELINE GMBH, COLOGNE

Location
more than 30 German cities

Client
Max-Planck-Gesellschaft zur Förderung der Wissenschaften e.V., Munich

Month / Year
June – September 2018

Duration
several months

Dramaturgy / Direction / Coordination
onliveline GmbH, Cologne

Media
Heinz Stricker media3 (Teaser video); MisterWissen2Go & Doktor Whatson (during campaign); onliveline & Teams (on Max Planck Day); Max-Planck-Zentrale & Institut

Music
Matz Flores

Artists / Show acts
Max Planck scientists from all Max Planck Institutes

Photos
Max-Planck-Gesellschaft, Munich

2018 fand der deutschlandweite Max-Planck-Tag mit gleich
drei Jubiläen parallel statt – dem 160. Geburtstag von Max
Planck, dem 100-jährigen Jubiläum seines Nobelpreises
und dem 70-jährigen Bestehen der Max-Planck-Gesellschaft. Um den Tag, die Jubiläen sowie die Sichtbarkeit
der Forschung an sich zu steigern, entwickelte onliveline
eine übergreifende Kampagne unter dem Namen
#wonachsuchstdu. Die recht allgemein gehaltene Ziel-
gruppe sollte spielerisch, interaktiv und nachhaltig mit dem
Thema Forschung in Kontakt kommen.

EINE FRAGEN-KAMPAGNE NUTZT JUBILÄEN UND DEN MAX-PLANCK-TAG ALS KATALYSATOR FÜR DIE AWARENESS AUF FORSCHUNG.

A QUESTION CAMPAIGN MAKES USE OF THE ANNIVERSARIES AND MAX PLANCK DAY AS A CATALYST OF THE AWARENESS OF SCIENCE.

In 2018, the Germany-wide Max Planck Day took place with
three parallel anniversary celebrations – the 160th birthday
of Max Planck, the 100-year anniversary of his Nobel Prize
and the 70-year existence of the Max Planck Society. In
order to highlight the day, the anniversaries and the visibi-
lity of the research, onliveline developed an overarching
campaign under the name #wonachsuchstdu (what are you
looking for). The rather general target group was to come
into contact with the theme of research in a playful, interactive and lasting manner.

Grundlage dafür war eine Online-Fragenkampagne, die die Max-Planck-Forscher mit ihren Fragen und Antworten sowie die Bandbreite der Max-Planck-Forschung vorstellte und gleichzeitig den Max-Planck-Tag einband. Über die Social-Media-Kanäle der Max-Planck-Gesellschaft, ihre 84 Institute und eine zentrale Website wurden die Menschen aufgefordert, selbst Fragen einzureichen. Zwei YouTuber besuchten die 16 Max-Planck-Institute, um Antworten auf die zahlreich eingereichten Fragen zu finden und zum deutschlandweiten Max-Planck-Tag einzuladen.

Zum Finale der Kampagne, dem Max-Planck-Tag, fanden in ganz Deutschland verschiedenste Events statt. Auf dem Münchner Marstallplatz liefen die Fäden aller Veranstaltungen zusammen und wurden durch einen Livestream medial erweitert. Die zuvor herumgereisten YouTuber bündelten die Highlights, luden zu direkten Gesprächen, verschiedenen Forschungsthemen und Science Slams. Ein „bunter Hashtag" war das symbolische Verbindungsstück zwischen allen Veranstaltungen und Online-Aktivitäten.

The basis for this was an online question campaign that presented the Max Planck researchers with their questions and answers, as well as the scope of Max Planck research, whilst incorporating the Max Planck Day. Through the social media channels of the Max Planck Society, its 84 institutes and a central website, people were encouraged to submit questions themselves. Two YouTubers visited the 16 Max Planck Institutes to find answers to the many submitted questions and to issue invitations to the Germany-wide Max Planck Day.

A wide variety of events were held throughout Germany for the finale of the campaign, the Max Planck Day. The threads of all the events came together at the Munich Marstallplatz and were extended by a media livestream. The previously travelling YouTubers gathered the highlights and gave out invitations to direct discussions, various research topics and science slams. A "colourful hashtag" was the symbolic connecting element between all the events and online activities.

LA FLÈCHE DANS LES NUAGES
ACTLD, BRUSSELS

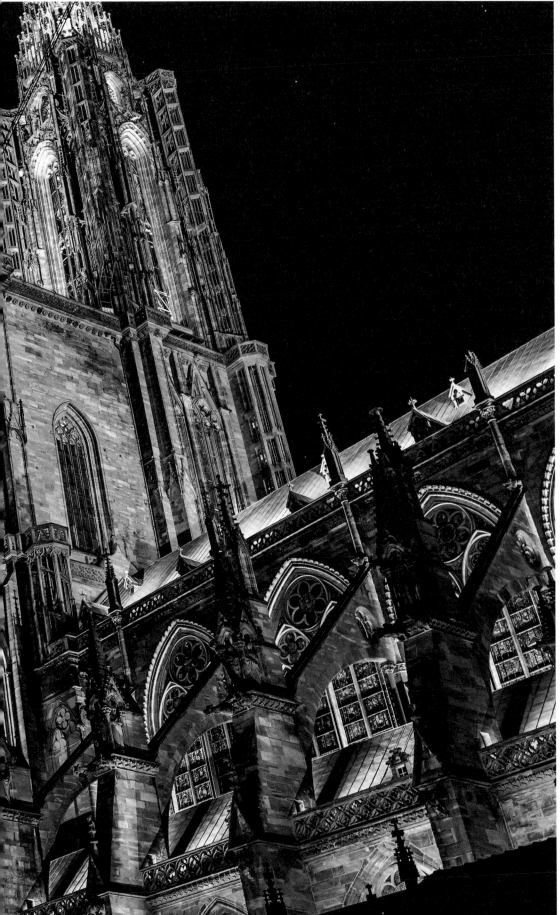

Location
Place du Chtâeau, Strasbourg

Client
City of Strasbourg

Month / Year
July – September 2018

Duration
8 weeks

Dramaturgy / Direction / Coordination / Graphics / Media / Films
ACTLD, Brussels

Architecture / Design / Construction
FL Structure, Offendorf

Music
Musicom, Brussels

Decoration
FX3, Beauvechain

Others
ADC Production, Zaventem (Video);
Lagoona, Strasbourg (Sound)

Photos
Frank Baudy

A PROJECTION ONTO THE SKY THAT RECALLED THE BOLD GOALS AND DREAMS OF THE MEDIEVAL BUILDING MASTERS.

Strasbourg cathedral was built between the 12th and 15th centuries. The exceptional building is now among the most significant cathedrals in European architectural history, as well as one of the largest sandstone buildings in the world. In the Middle Ages, the 142-metre-high tower was the highest manmade building. It is hardly surprising that the city of Strasburg regularly celebrates its cathedral, for example with extensive public mapping projects. This was also the case in the year 2018, but this time ACT Lighting Design thought up something new.

Das Straßburger Münster wurde zwischen dem 12. und 15. Jahrhundert erbaut. Der außergewöhnliche Bau zählt heute zu den bedeutendsten Kathedralen der europäischen Architekturgeschichte sowie zu den größten Sandsteinbauten der Welt. Im Mittelalter war der 142 Meter hohe Turm lange Zeit das höchste von Menschen geschaffene Bauwerk. Nicht verwunderlich, dass die Stadt Straßburg ihr Münster regelmäßig zum Beispiel mit aufwendigen öffentlichen Mappingprojekten feiern lässt. So auch im Jahr 2018. Doch diesmal hatte sich ACT Lighting Design etwas Neues einfallen lassen.

Thema sollte die finale Bauzeit des Turms zwischen dem 14. und 15. Jahrhundert sein. Zu dieser Zeit war der Place du Château neben dem Münster eine gigantische Baustelle. Zahlreiche Bauarbeiter schnitten Steine, schmiedeten Metall und entwickelten für damalige Zeiten innovativste Hubmaschinen und Baugerüste. Dass dieses einem Wunder gleichende Bauvorhaben tatsächlich realisiert wurde, ist den Baumeistern und mittelalterlichen Architekten Ulrich und Hultz zu verdanken. Es waren vor allem Hultz und seine Verrücktheit, die die Grenzen der Vorstellung und damaligen Technik immer wieder vorantrieben.

EINE PROJEKTION AM HIMMEL, DIE AN DIE WAGEMUTIGEN ZIELE UND TRÄUME DER MITTELALTERLICHEN BAUMEISTER ERINNERTE.

The theme was the final building construction period of the tower, between the 14th and 15th century. At that time, the Place du Château, next to the cathedral, was a gigantic building site. Many builders cut stone, forged metal and developed the most innovative lifting machines and building scaffolding of the time. The fact that this miraculous construction project was actually realised is thanks to the building masters and medieval architects Ulrich and Hultz. It was especially Hultz and his craziness that kept driving the boundaries of the imagination and of the technical methods of the time forwards.

Um diese Baugeschichte auf dem Originalschauplatz nachzuerzählen, nutzte ACTLD ein neues Mappingkonzept: das Video Netting. Mitten über dem Place du Château wurde ein 400 Quadratmeter großes Netz gespannt, das als Projektionsfläche diente und es ermöglichte, eine Geschichte „an den Himmel" zu projizieren. Das öffentliche Event namens „La Flèche dans les Nuages", übersetzt „Der Pfeil in den Wolken", lud die Öffentlichkeit dazu ein, die verschiedenen Protagonisten dieser technischen, künstlerischen und menschlichen Geschichte auf neue Weise zu entdecken.

In order to recount this building history on the original site, ACTLD used a new mapping concept: video netting. Right in the middle over the Place du Château, a 400-square-metre large net was stretched that served as a projection surface and allowed the projection of a story "onto the sky". The public event called "La Flèche dans les Nuages", which translates as "The Arrow in the Clouds", invited the public to discover the various protagonists of this technical, artistic and human period of history in a novel way.

INSIDEOUT | LA CASA AZUL
FLORA&FAUNAVISIONS GMBH, BERLIN

Location
Dubai Art Week 2018

Client
Dubai Art Week & INKED

Month / Year
March 2018

Duration
several days

Dramaturgy / Direction / Coordination
StudioLeighSachwitz

**Architecture / Design / Graphics /
Lighting / Media / Film**
flora&faunavisions GmbH, Berlin

Music
Andi Toma (Mouse on Mars)

Decoration / Equipment / Catering
INKED, Dubai

Realisation
One Union Exhibitions

Others
*Neumann&Müller GmbH & Co. KG,
Esslingen am Neckar (Technology)*

Photos
*diephotodesigner.de; flora&faunavisions,
Berlin; INKED*

Die Multimedia-Installation „INSIDEOUT" wurde 2015 von flora&faunavisions und StudioLeighSachwitz entworfen. Das multisensorische Erlebnis beschreibt in seinen Ursprüngen das Haus als einen sicheren Hafen, um uns vor den Naturgewalten zu beschützen. Besucher können den projizierten Regen auf dem Dach, dunkle Wolken durch das Fenster und das finale „reinigende" Mondlicht beobachten. Das dazugehörige Sounddesign stammt von dem preisgekrönten Komponisten, Musiker und Produzenten Andi Toma.

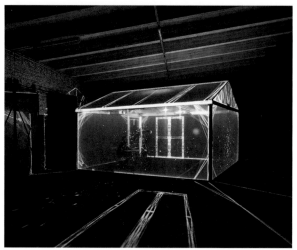

EIN INTENSIVES DINNER-ERLEBNIS INMITTEN EINER MULTISENSORISCHEN INSTALLATION AUS PROJEKTIONEN UND KLANG.

The multimedia installation "INSIDEOUT" was designed by flora&flaunavisions and StudioLeighSachwitz in 2015. The multisensory experience describes the origins of the house as a safe haven to protect us from natural forces. Visitors can observe the projected rain on the roof, dark clouds through the window and the final "cleansing" moonlight. The accompanying sound design is by the award-winning composer, musician and producer Andi Toma.

Auf der Dubai Art Week 2018 entwickelte flora&faunavisions eine neue Version der Installation in Verbindung mit einer Pop-Up-Dinnerserie: „INSIDEOUT | La Casa Azul". Inspiriert von Frida Kahlo, einer der bedeutendsten Künstlerinnen und Frauen des 20. Jahrhunderts, entstanden fünf neue Szenarien und Projektionen. Sie führten durch Frida Kahlos dramatisches Leben und sollten gemeinsam mit einem Fünf-Gänge-Menü die Emotionen und Sinne der Besucher anregen. Die Multimedia-Installation „INSIDEOUT" war während der Dubai Art Week für die Öffentlichkeit zugänglich, die Veranstaltung „La Casa Azul" mit dem intensiven Dinner-Erlebnis fand in deren Rahmen mehrmals statt.

AN INTENSIVE DINNER EXPERIENCE AMIDST A MULTISENSORY INSTALLATION CONSISTING OF PROJECTIONS AND SOUND.

At the Dubai Art Week 2018, flora&faunavisions developed a new version of the installation in connection with a pop-up dinner series: "INSIDEOUT | La Casa Azul". Inspired by Frida Kahlo, one of the most significant female artists and women of the 20th century, five new scenarios and projections were created. They led through Frida Kahlo's dramatic life and were designed to stimulate the emotions and senses of the visitors with a five-course menu. The multimedia installation "INSIDEOUT" was accessible to the public during the Dubai Art Week, which offered the event "La Casa Azul" with its intensive dinner experience on several dates.

RED BULL MUSIC / KMN GANG
DREINULL AGENTUR FÜR MEDIATAINMENT
GMBH & CO. KG, BERLIN

Location
Prinzessinnenstraße 23, Berlin

Client
Red Bull Deutschland GmbH

Month / Year
July 2018

Duration
1 day

Dramaturgy / Graphics
Red Bull Music, Glutamat Berlin,
DREINULL, Berlin

Direction / Coordination
DREINULL, Berlin; Glutamat, Berlin

Architecture / Design
DREINULL, Berlin

Lighting
Lautwerfer, Berlin

Film
Glutamat, Berlin

Music / Artists / Show acts
KMN Gang

Realisation
Gehrke Event- und Tourmanagement, Berlin;
Matthias Westebbe, Berlin

Photos
Dirk Mathesius, Berlin; dieserbobby

Ein Event muss schon länger nicht mehr alleine die Gäste vor Ort begeistern. Eines der wichtigsten Ziele ist das Erreichen von Menschen über das Event hinaus. Medienresonanz, ob in Social Media, Blogs oder Zeitschriften, ist mindestens genauso wichtig – in manchen Fällen sogar noch wichtiger. Ein Marketingevent sollte daher auch immer für spannende Inhalte oder ein „Big Picture" sorgen, die sich im Sinne der Public Relations einsetzen lassen. Kaum ein Unternehmen hat das so verinnerlicht wie Red Bull.

For a considerable time, an event has not only been about enthusing the guests on site. One of the most important objectives is to reach people beyond the event. Media resonance, whether on social media, blogs or magazines, is at least just as important – in some cases even more important. A marketing event should therefore always ensure interesting content or a "wider picture" that can be used in the interests of public relations. Red Bull has internalised this like scarcely any other company.

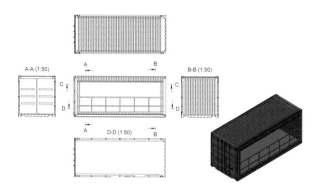

EINE BÜHNE IN 21,2 METER HÖHE – MIT DEM ZIEL, REKORDE ZU BRECHEN UND FÜR MEDIENRESONANZ ZU SORGEN.

Gemeinsam mit DREINULL wollte Red Bull Music diesmal mit einem neuen Rekord für Aufsehen und mit einem geheimnisvollen Countdown für Spannung sorgen. Der erste in den Red Bull Music Studios Berlin aufgenommene Track der Deutschrap-Crew KMN Gang sollte gefeiert werden. Direkt nach dem Release von *KMN Member* startete in den Social Channels der Rapper ein Countdown zum 4. Juli 2018. Weitere Informationen dazu gab es nicht. Erst mit Ablauf des Countdowns erfuhren Fans, wo die Gang zu finden sei. Schnell fanden sich rund 500 Menschen ein und beobachteten, wie ein zur Bühne umfunktionierter Container in 21,2 Meter Höhe gehoben wurde. Auf dieser Bühne, der bis dahin höchsten weltweit, gab die KMN Gang ihre neuesten Songs zum Besten. Zurück auf dem Boden, folgte ein Überraschungskonzert für die spontan zusammengekommenen Zuschauer.

Together with DREINULL, this time Red Bull Music wanted to draw attention by breaking a record and to create excitement with a mysterious countdown. The first track by German rap crew KMN Gang recorded at Red Bull Music Studios Berlin was to be celebrated. Immediately after the release of KMN Member, a countdown to 4 July 2019 was launched on the social channels of the rappers. There was no further information about it. It was only as the countdown unfolded that fans discovered where the gang was to be found. Very soon 500 people gathered and watched how a container converted into a stage was lifted 21.2 metres high, the highest stage worldwide thus far, on which KMN Gang performed their latest songs. Back on the ground, a surprise concert followed for the spontaneous gathering of spectators.

A STAGE 21.2 METRES HIGH – WITH THE AIM OF BREAKING RECORDS AND ENSURING MEDIA RESONANCE.

WM POP-UP STORE
UNIPLAN GMBH & CO. KG, SHANGHAI

Location
Shenzhen, Beijing, Chengdu, Shanghai,
Xi'an, Jinan, Hangzhou, Suzhou, Tianjin,
Wuhan, Zhengzhou, Qingdao

Client
WM MOTOR, Shanghai

Month / Year
August 2018 – January 2019

Duration
6 months

**Dramaturgy / Direction / Coordination /
Architecture / Design / Graphics / Film /
Music / Decoration**
Uniplan GmbH & Co. KG, Shanghai

Lighting / Realisation / Construction
Spoondrift Exhibition & Events Shanghai
Co. Ltd.

Media
Trustwin Group

Catering
TC Coffee

Photos
CHONG VISION International Photography
Co. Ltd., Beijing

EIN POP-UP-EISHAUS PRÄSENTIERT DEN NEUEN ELEKTRO-SUV UND MACHT AUF DEN KLIMAWANDEL AUFMERKSAM.

Der EX5 ist ein elektrischer Kompakt-Crossover-SUV, der vom chinesischen Elektroautohersteller Weltmeister hergestellt wird. Für die Einführung der neuen Marke und die Vorstellung des ersten Produkts für den chinesischen Markt sollte ein Pop-up-Store entwickelt werden. Er sollte sich an ein jüngeres Publikum richten und für Gesprächsstoff sorgen. Ziel war es, sich mit einer künstlerischen und inhaltlichen Kampagne von anderen Automobilherstellern abzuheben.

The EX5 is an electric compact crossover SUV made by the Chinese electric car manufacturer Weltmeister. A pop-up store was to be developed to introduce the new brand and present the first product for the Chinese market. It was to target a younger public and provide a topic of conversation. The aim was to stand out from other automobile manufacturers with an artistic campaign rich in content.

A POP-UP ICE HOUSE PRESENTS THE NEW ELECTRIC SUV AND DRAWS ATTENTION TO CLIMATE CHANGE.

Uniplan ließ sich vom Nordlicht inspirieren und entwickelte eine Art „Eishaus". Eingebettet in Szenerien aus kühlem Eis und gemütlichem Hygge-Flair präsentierte man der Öffentlichkeit den neuen Wagen. Die Gestaltung bezog die Farben der Marke ein und realisierte eine Sommer- und Winterversion. Inhaltlich wurde die Wagenpräsentation in eine Geschichte eingebettet, die das Bewusstsein für die Auswirkungen der globalen Erwärmung schärfen und den Übergang in eine neue Ära der Elektroautos verdeutlichen sollte. Ein kurzes Video brachte die Besucher zum Nordpol, ließ sie dem Klang schmelzender Gletscher lauschen und erzählte von den Problemen der Eisbären. Hierbei arbeitete die Automobilmarke mit NGOs zusammen. Inhalte, Fotos und Videos wurden über den offiziellen WeChat-Kanal sowie mithilfe von Fans und Influencern kommuniziert.

Uniplan was inspired by Nordlicht and developed a type of "ice house". Embedded in settings of cool ice and a cozy Hygge flair, the new car was presented to the public. Its design incorporated the colours of the brand and realised a summer and winter version. In terms of content, the car presentation was integrated into a story designed to raise awareness of the effects of global warming and show the transition to a new era of electric cars. A brief video took the visitors to the North Pole, let them listen to the sound of melting glaciers and told of the problems faced by polar bears. For this purpose, the automobile brand cooperated with NGOs. Content, photos and videos were communicated through the official WeChat channel as well as with the help of fans and influencers.

NATURE BOX @ GLOW –
THE BEAUTY CONVENTION
STAGG & FRIENDS GMBH, DUSSELDORF

Location
STATION Berlin

Client
Henkel AG & Co. KGaA /
Henkel Beauty Care

Month / Year
October 2018

Duration
several days

Dramaturgy / Direction / Coordination /
Architecture / Design / Graphics / Music
STAGG & FRIENDS GmbH, Dusseldorf

Lighting / Decoration / Realisation
artlife GmbH, Hofheim am Taunus

Photos
Paul Aidan Perry, Berlin

Nicht nur Marken möchten zum Thema in den sozialen Netzwerken werden. Auch Messe- und Eventbesucher suchen nach Momenten, die sich zur Selbstinszenierung bei Instagram & Co. anbieten. Ein wichtiger Aspekt, der nicht nur Besucher anlockt und begeistert, sondern gleichzeitig dabei hilft, ein Marketingevent online zu verbreiten. Eine solche Strategie muss jedoch bereits in der Eventkonzeption sowie in alle Design- und Inszenierungsdetails einbezogen werden – und nicht erst in der Kommunikation. Es gilt, Erlebnisse zu schaffen, die die Markenwerte kommunizieren und gleichzeitig „instagramable" sind.

MARKENERLEBNISSE UND FOTO-SPOTS SOLLEN BEGEISTERN UND OPTIMALE SOCIAL-MEDIA-BILD-MOMENTE LIEFERN.

BRAND EXPERIENCES AND PHOTO SPOTS ARE DESIGNED TO BE APPEALING AND TO PROVIDE OPTIMAL SOCIAL MEDIA PHOTO MOMENTS.

It is not only brands that want to be talked about on social networks. Trade fair and event visitors also look for moments that lend themselves to self-presentations on Instagram & co. This is an important aspect that not only draws and enthuses visitors but also helps to spread a marketing event online. However, such a strategy must already be incorporated in the event conception, as well as in all design and staging details – not just in its communication. It is about creating experiences that communicate the brand values and are at the same time "instagramable".

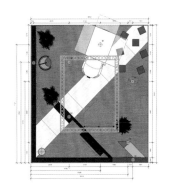

Einen solchen Ansatz verfolgte STAGG & FRIENDS für die neue Marke Nature Box von Henkel auf der Beauty Convention GLOW 2018. Foto-Spots, Aktivierungsmöglichkeiten sowie Influencer-Marketing-Tools sollten sowohl die 12.000 Beautybegeisterten vor Ort als auch Social-Media-Follower begeistern. Im Zentrum der Foto-Spots stand ein 2,5 Meter hoher und 6 Meter breiter Vertical Garden aus echten Pflanzen. Unterschiedliche Selfie-Spots sollten natürliche Schönheit spielerisch ins richtige Licht rücken. „Foto-Gimmicks" und fünf Ölsäulen, die in den Farben der Produktlinien sprudelten, griffen die Thematik und Hashtags der Marke auf. So sollten nicht nur optimale Bildmomente geboten, sondern auch Live-Stories bei Instagram gefördert werden.

STAGG & FRIENDS pursued such an approach for Henkel's new brand Nature Box at the Beauty Convention GLOW in 2018. Photo spots, activation possibilities and influencer marketing tools were designed to appeal to both the 12,000 beauty enthusiasts on site and social media followers. At the centre of the photo spots was a 2.5-metre-high and 6-metre-wide vertical garden with real plants. Various selfie spots were to cast the right light on natural beauty in a playful manner. "Photo gimmicks" and five oil columns that bubbled the colours of the product lines took up the themes and hashtags of the brand. This was intended not only to offer optimal photographic moments but also to promote live stories on Instagram.

MONNEM BIKE – WHERE IT ALL BEGAN
OTTOMISU COMMUNICATION GMBH, HEIDELBERG

Location
Mannheim, City area

Client
*City of Mannheim / City planning
Department*

Year
2017

Duration
several months

**Dramaturgy / Graphics / Artists /
Show acts**
ottomisu communication GmbH, Heidelberg

**Direction / Coordination / Architecture /
Design / Lighting / Media / Film / Music /
Decoration / Realisation**
*ottomisu communication GmbH, Heidelberg;
City of Mannheim*

Others
*m:con GmbH, Mannheim (City festival
support)*

Photos
*ottomisu communication GmbH, Heidelberg;
City of Mannheim*

Das Fahrrad wurde 1817 von Karl Drais in Mannheim erfunden. 2017 beging diese Erfindung ihr 200. Jubiläum, das die Stadt Mannheim mit einer Abschlussshow und verschiedenen Aktivitäten feiern wollte. Ottomisu entwickelte für diesen Anlass nicht nur eine Show, sondern eine ganzheitliche Kampagne, die die Mannheimer Bürger einband und das Fahrrad als regionale Erfindung bewusst machte. Kommunikativer Ausgangspunkt war eine neu entwickelte Marke mit regionalem Bezug: „MONNEM BIKE".

ANSTATT EINES JUBILÄUMS FÜR DIE MENSCHEN ENTSTAND EINE GANZHEITLICHE KAMPAGNE MIT DEN MENSCHEN.

The bicycle was invented in 1817 by Karl Drais in Mannheim. In 2017, this invention had its 200th anniversary, which the city of Mannheim wanted to celebrate with a final show and various activities. For this occasion, Ottomisu developed not only a show but an overarching campaign that incorporated the Mannheim citizens and drew attention to the bicycle as a regional invention. The communicative starting point was a newly developed brand with a regional reference: "MONNEM BIKE".

The activities were begun by a project and ideas competition. Citizens and local initiatives, societies and companies could submit projects and ideas on the topic of bicycles. The winners were selected by public voting, given awards and supported with prize money between 1000 and 4000 Euros. Small and large projects were thus initiated that infused the brand "MONNEM BIKE" with life and helped to draw attention to the anniversary.

Den Anfang der Aktivitäten bildete ein Projekt- bzw. Ideenwettbewerb. Bürgerinnen und Bürger sowie lokale Initiativen, Vereine und Unternehmen konnten Projekte und Ideen zum Thema Fahrrad einreichen. Via Public Voting wurden die Gewinner gewählt, prämiert und mit Preisgeldern zwischen 1.000 und 4.000 Euro bei der Umsetzung unterstützt. So wurden kleine und große Projekte angestoßen, die die Marke „MONNEM BIKE" mit Leben füllten und dem Jubiläum zu Aufmerksamkeit verhalfen.

Die Stadt Mannheim entschied sich daraufhin, weitere geplante Events und Aktionen unter der Dachmarke „MONNEM BIKE" zu veranstalten – darunter ein durch Pedale angetriebenes Fahrradkino, ein internationaler Fachkongress, viele Ausstellungen, eine Gala mit Politprominenz und ein großes Stadtfest zum eigentlichen Geburtstag. Das Finale bildete eine Show mit allen Beteiligten. Inhaltlich nahm die multimediale Inszenierung Bezug zu den vergangenen 200 Jahren, widmete sich aber mehrheitlich den zukünftigen Facetten und Chancen des Fahrrads. Eine Landingpage bündelte alle Aktivitäten, bot Informations- und Interaktionsmöglichkeiten und streute die Kampagne mithilfe von Facebook, YouTube und Instagram.

INSTEAD OF AN ANNIVERSARY FOR THE PEOPLE, AN OVERARCHING CAMPAIGN WAS CREATED WITH THE PEOPLE.

The city of Mannheim then decided to hold further events and incentives under the "MONNEM BIKE" banner – including a bicycle cinema driven by pedals, an international specialist congress, many exhibitions, a gala with political VIPs and a big municipal festival on the actual anniversary day. The finale was a show with all those involved. In terms of content, the multimedia staging referred to the past 200 years but was mostly dedicated to future facets and potential of the bicycle. A landing page pooled all the activities, offered information and interaction possibilities and spread the campaign with the help of Facebook, YouTube and Instagram.

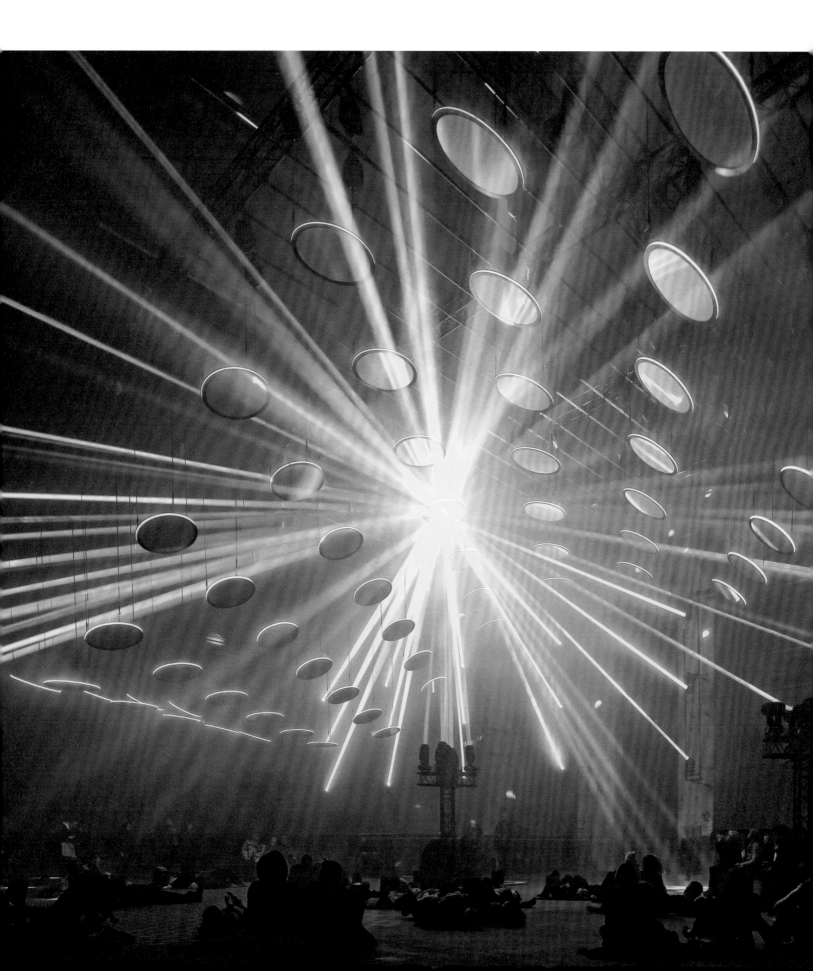

SKALAR
WHITEVOID GMBH, BERLIN

Location
Kraftwerk Berlin

Month / Year
January – February 2018

Duration
1 month

Awards
Winner at dark awards 2018

Dramaturgy
Christopher Bauder (WHITEvoid, Berlin)

**Direction / Coordination / Architecture /
Design / Graphics / Lighting / Media /
Decoration / Overall**
WHITEvoid, Berlin

Music
Kangding Ray, Berlin

Artists / Show acts
*Christopher Bauder, Berlin; Kangding Ray,
Berlin*

Rigging
*satis&fy AG, Berlin; Lichtblick Bühnen-
technik GmbH, Berlin*

Partners / Produced by
*WHITEvoid GmbH, Kraftwerk Berlin,
CTM Festival*

Equipment
*Kinetic system by KINETIC LIGHTS,
Moving lights by ROBE*

Photos
Ralph Larmann, Hadamar

Das von Lichtkünstler Christopher Bauder und Musiker Kangding Ray ins Leben gerufene „Skalar – Reflections on Light and Sound" ist die neueste Produktion von WHITE-void. Die audiovisuelle Installation kombiniert die für die Künstler typischen Elemente aus kinetischen Objekten, Licht und monumentalem Klang. Neu ist bei dieser Installation die Umlenkung von Lichtstrahlen, sodass sie nicht nur einen linearen Anfang und ein Ende haben. Mithilfe beweglicher Spiegel ist es gelungen, Lichtstrahlen zu reflektieren und gleichzeitig auf einen gezielten Punkt auszurichten. Licht wird so als festes Material behandelt, das architektonisch geformt werden kann und eine 45 Meter lange, 20 Meter breite und 10 Meter hohe Lichtstruktur bildet.

"Skalar – Reflections on Light and Sound" created by light artist Christopher Bauder and musician Kangding Ray is the latest production by WHITEvoid. The audiovisual installation combines the elements of kinetic objects, light and monumental sound that are typical of the artists. The new feature of this installation is the redirection of beams of light so that they do not have just a linear start and end. By means of movable mirrors, they succeeded in reflecting beams of light and at the same time directing them towards a targeted point. Light is therefore treated as a solid material that can be architecturally shaped, forming a light structure 45 metres long, 20 metres wide and 10 metres high.

EINE MONUMENTALE INSTALLATION ALS INTENSIVE REISE DURCH DIE GRUNDLEGENDEN MENSCHLICHEN EMOTIONEN.

Inhaltlich soll Skalar eine intensive Reise durch den Zyklus grundlegender menschlicher Emotionen sein. Emotionen wie Ehrfurcht, Überraschung, Heiterkeit und Vorfreude werden durch ständig wechselnde Tonalitäten von Licht, Ton und Bewegung ausgelöst. Durch wiederkehrende Zyklen und die teils bewusste Überforderung der Sinne entsteht ein kollektives und zugleich individuelles Erlebnis. Anfang 2018 wurde Skalar im Kraftwerk Berlin im Rahmen des CTM Festival for Adventurous Music and Art ins Leben gerufen. Enstanden ist eine monumentale Erzählung aus 65 kinetischen Spiegeln, 90 synchronisierten Lichtstrahlen und einem ausgefeilten Multikanal-Soundsystem.

In terms of content, Skalar is intended to be an intensive journey through the cycle of fundamental human emotions. Emotions such as reverence, surprise, cheerfulness and anticipation are triggered by means of constantly changing tonalities of light, sound and movement. Through recurring cycles and the partly conscious overloading of the senses, a collective and at the same time individual experience is created. In early 2018, Skalar was launched at the Kraftwerk Berlin power plant as part of the CTM festival for Adventurous Music and Art. The result is a monumental narrative comprising 65 kinetic mirrors, 90 synchronised beams of light and a sophisticated multichannel sound system.

A MONUMENTAL INSTALLATION AS AN INTENSIVE JOURNEY THROUGH FUNDAMENTAL HUMAN EMOTIONS.

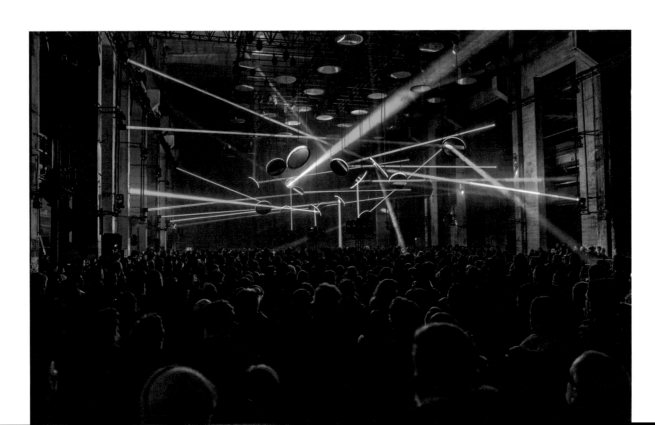

ADIDAS ORIGINALS X FALCON @ B&&B
DREINULL AGENTUR FÜR MEDIATAINMENT
GMBH & CO. KG, BERLIN

Location
Arena Berlin

Client
*adidas AG / adidas Originals, Herzogen-
aurach*

Month / Year
August–September 2018

Duration
3 days

**Dramaturgy / Direction / Coordination /
Architecture / Design / Graphics**
DREINULL, Berlin

Lighting
PAM Events, Berlin

Film
Selam X, Berlin

Music / Artists / Show acts
MØ

Decoration / Equipment / Realisation
Balloni, Berlin

Photos
Leni Paperboats; Jana Theresa Lou, Berlin

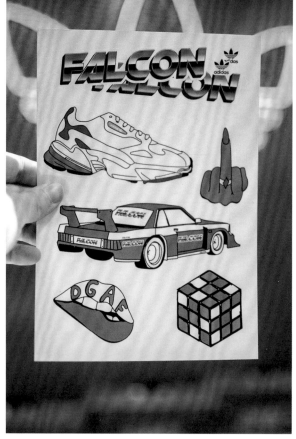

EINE GESTALTERISCHE UND THEMATISCHE REISE IN DIE FEMINISTISCH GEPRÄGTEN 90ER-JAHRE.

Die 90er-Jahre sind in der Streetwear-Branche ein nach wie vor stilbildendes Thema. Für den retro-neuen adidas-Damen-Sneaker „Originals Falcon W" entwickelte DREINULL daher ein ikonografisches 90er-Jahre-Setting auf der Bread && Butter 2018. Dabei drehte sich das Konzept nicht allein um die knallige Ästhetik dieser Zeit, sondern auch um die damalige Bewegung unter dem Begriff „Dritte Welle".

The 1990s continue to be a theme that shapes style in the streetwear sector. For the retro-new adidas ladies' trainers "Originals Falcon W", DREINULL therefore developed an iconographic 90s setting at Bread && Butter 2018. The concept revolved not only around the brash aesthetics of that time but also around the movement under the notion of "Third Wave".

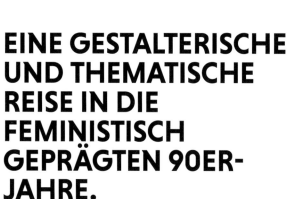

A CREATIVE AND THEMATIC JOURNEY INTO THE 90S CHARACTERISED BY FEMINISM.

Das räumliche Setting erzählte die Geschichte der Falcon-Tuning-Werkstatt. Ein in Pink und Türkis gehaltener Mercedes 190 und ein BMW-Motorrad zwischen neonbeleuchteten Alufelgen und Chromdisplays ließen den unverkennbaren Stil der Zeit aufleben. Das begleitende Programm thematisierte Selbstvertrauen, weibliche Selbstbestimmung, Inspiration und Ikonen der 90er-Jahre. Die dänische Musikerin MØ bot eine intime Performance, die man hautnah miterleben konnte, und beteiligte sich zusammen mit Slavka Jancikova (Global Category Director for Women's Footwear), HYPEBAE-Redakteurin Nav Gill und Moderatorin Wana Limar an einem Panel. Als Instagram-Spot diente ein Motorrad vor bewegtem bonbonfarbenem Himmel. Für den passenden Look der 90er sorgte das angebotene Style-Tuning mit Nail Art, Braids und, für die Mutigsten, Piercings. Den passenden Rahmen boten Streetfood-Angebote der Messe sowie über 40 weitere Streetwear-Brands-Pop-Ups, die sich als Spätkauf, eine Hommage an die Berliner U-Bahn oder ein Donut Diner inszenierten.

The spatial setting told the story of the Falcon tuning workshop. A Mercedes 190 in pink and turquoise and a BMW motorbike between neon illuminated aluminium wheel rims and chrome displays brought the unmistakable style of the era to life. The accompanying programme thematised self-confidence, female self-determination, inspiration and icons of the 90s. The Danish musician MØ offered a private performance making close contact with her audience and participated in a panel together with Slavka Jancikova (Global Category Director for Women's Footwear), HYPEBAE editor Nav Gill and hostess Wana Limar. A motorbike in front of a turbulent sweet-coloured sky served as an Instagram spot. The presented style tuning with nail art, braids and, for the most daring, piercings, ensured a suitable 90s look. Streetfood options and more than 40 additional streetwear brand pop-ups, presented as open-late convenience stores, an homage to the Berlin underground or a donut diner provided a suitable setting.

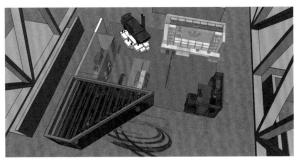

LICHTFESTIVAL 2018
STUDIONOW GMBH, BERLIN

Location
Swarovski Kristallwelten, Wattens

Client
*Swarovski Kristallwelten / D. Swarovski
Tourism Services GmbH*

Month / Year
January – February 2018

Duration
1 month

Awards
Silver at Austrian Event Award

Lead / CD / Architecture / Design
StudioNOW GmbH, Berlin

Direction
onliveline GmbH, Cologne

Lighting
Björn Hermann Lichtdesign, Berlin

Music
*Matt Flores (Composition); Hansjörg Wenzel
(360° Sound Design)*

Others
*PRG Production Resource Group AG
(Technology)*

Photos
Sandra Sommerkamp

Mit den Swarovski Kristallwelten ist es gelungen, eine der meistgesehenen Sehenswürdigkeiten Österreichs inmitten der Tiroler Berglandschaft zu schaffen. Die 1995 von André Heller konzipierte Erlebniswelt besteht aus einer weitläufigen Parklandschaft und einem Kunstmuseum, die ihre Besucher erstaunen und begeistern sollen. Im Januar und Februar 2018 galt es, die Attraktivität und Bekanntheit der Kristallwelten durch ein neues, zeitlich begrenztes Angebot noch weiter zu steigern. So entstand die Idee eines Lichtfestivals, das die vorhandene Parklandschaft mit Licht und Klang überraschend neu in Szene setzte.

EINE SPEKTAKULÄRE LICHTSHOW MIT DEM ZIEL, DIE KRISTALLWELTEN NOCH ATTRAKTIVER UND BEKANNTER ZU MACHEN.

A SPECTACULAR LIGHT SHOW WITH THE AIM OF MAKING THE CRYSTAL WORLDS EVEN MORE ATTRACTIVE AND WELL-KNOWN.

The Swarovski Crystal Worlds succeeded in creating one of Austria's most visited sightseeing attractions amidst the Tyrolean mountain landscape. The world of experience conceived by André Heller in 1995 consists of a spacious park and an art museum designed to amaze and enthral those who see it. In January and February 2018, the attractiveness and renown of the Crystal Worlds were to be increased even further by means of a new feature for a limited time. This sparked the idea of a light festival that set a surprising new scene for the existing park landscape using light and sound.

StudioNOW entwickelte ein Konzept, das von einer magischen Welt erzählte. Inhaltlich präsentierte man die Geschichte des Riesen, der zentralen Figur der Kristallwelten, der von seinen Weltreisen und Abenteuern träumt. Jeder Akt der Show war einer dieser verrückten, lebhaften und dramatischen Träume mit sprechenden Tieren, magischen Augen, Riesen und Zwergen, Einhörnern, Hexen, Clowns und Medizinmännern. Internationale Licht-, Medien- und Klangkünstler erschufen dafür eine spektakuläre audiovisuelle Show. Die bestehenden Parkelemente wurden um dramaturgische, erzählerische und multimediale Bestandteile ergänzt und ließen eine Wunderwelt entstehen, in der Traum und Wirklichkeit miteinander verschmelzen. Als Highlight wurde ein 33 Meter hohes Riesenrad mit 400.000 LEDs installiert und in die Inszenierung eingebunden.

StudioNOW developed a concept that told of a magical world. Its content presented the story of the giant, the central figure of the Crystal Worlds, who dreams of his world travels and adventures. Each act of the show was one of these crazy, lively and dramatic dreams with talking animals, magic eyes, giants and dwarves, unicorns, witches, clowns and medicine men. International light, media and sound artists created a spectacular audiovisual show for this. The existing park elements were extended by means of dramatic, narrative and multimedia components designed to give life to a wonderworld in which dream and reality become one. As a highlight, an over 33-metre-high big wheel illuminated by 400,000 LED lights was installed and incorporated into the setting.

HIGHLIGHT INNENSTADT
RAUMKONTAKT GMBH, KARLSRUHE

Location
Karlsruhe City centre (changing locations)

Client
City of Karlsruhe

Month / Year
October 2018 – December 2019

Duration
14 months

Direction / Coordination / Architecture / Design / Graphics / Lighting / Media / Realisation
raumkontakt GmbH, Karlsruhe

Photos
raumkontakt GmbH, Karlsruhe

Unter dem Titel „Zukunft Innenstadt" hat die Stadt Karlsruhe in den letzten Jahren verschiedene Maßnahmen realisiert und geplant – von konkreten infrastrukturellen Maßnahmen bis hin zu neu entwickelten Formaten. Doch wie kommuniziert man Geplantes und Erreichtes den Bürgerinnen und Bürgern? Wie begeistert man Menschen für die oft unsichtbaren Ziele, Pläne und Maßnahmen? Raumkontakt entwickelte für diese Fragestellungen ein pointiertes und aufsehenerregendes Kommunikationskonzept.

ÜBERDIMENSIONALE TISCHLEUCHTEN MACHEN AUF STÄDTISCHE PROJEKTE AUFMERKSAM – UND WERDEN ZUM IDEALEN FOTOMOTIV.

Under the title "Zukunft Innenstadt" (City Centre Future), the city of Karlsruhe has realised and planned various initiatives in recent years – from concrete infrastructural measures to newly developed formats. But how does one communicate what has been planned and achieved to the citizens? How does one enthuse people for the goals, plans and measures that are often invisible? Raumkontakt developed a pointed and attention-drawing communication concept in answer to these questions.

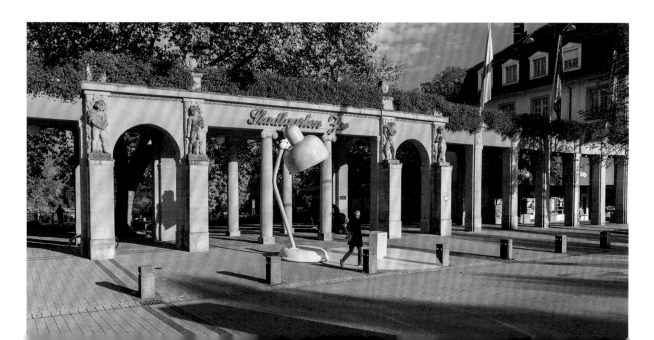

OVERSIZED TABLE LAMPS DRAW ATTENTION TO MUNICIPAL PROJECTS – AND BECOME AN IDEAL PHOTO MOTIF.

Überdimensionale viereinhalb Meter hohe Tischleuchten markierten mit gelben Lichtspots Orte und Aspekte der Innenstadtentwicklung und machten sichtbar, was neu, wissens- und entdeckungswürdig ist. Alle drei Monate wechselten sie ihren Standort und beleuchteten eine andere Maßnahme der Stadt. Dabei machten die Lampen nicht nur auf die jeweiligen Aktionen und Projekte aufmerksam, sie wurden selbst zum Hingucker und idealen Fotomotiv. Blogs, Presseberichte und soziale Netzwerke griffen die charmante Kampagne verständlicherweise schnell auf. Unter dem Label „Highlight Innenstadt" wurden ergänzende Ausstellungs- und Leitsysteme mit dem Projekt verbunden.

Oversized table lamps 4 $^1/_2$ metres high marked places and aspects of the city centre development with yellow light spots and made visible what was new, worth knowing and exploring. Every three months they changed their location and illuminated another municipal initiative. The lamps did not only draw attention to the respective initiatives and projects, they became an eye-catcher and ideal photo motif in their own right. Blogs, media reports and social networks understandably took up the charming campaign quickly. Under the label "City Centre Highlight", additional exhibition and guidance systems were combined with the project.

PORSCHE SOUND NACHT 2018
STAGG & FRIENDS GMBH, DUSSELDORF

Location
Porsche-Arena, Stuttgart

Client
Dr. Ing. h.c. F. Porsche AG, Stuttgart

Month / Year
October 2018

Duration
1 day

Awards
Finalist at International Advertising
Competition Golden Award of Montreux
2019

**Dramaturgy / Direction / Coordination /
Architecture / Design**
STAGG & FRIENDS GmbH, Dusseldorf

Graphics / Film
Dr. Ing. h.c. F. Porsche AG, Stuttgart

Lighting
Neumann&Müller GmbH & Co. KG,
Esslingen am Neckar

Music / Artists / Show acts
wolf one GmbH, Frechen

Decoration / Realisation
metron Vilshofen GmbH, Vilshofen

Photos
Markus Leser; Markus Pöhlmann,
Wolf Production GmbH, Frechen-Königsdorf

Die „Porsche Sound Nacht" fand bereits sieben Mal in Stuttgart statt. Bisher im Porsche Museum auf einer kleinen Bühne, ohne Fahraktivitäten und mit einer Anzahl von 911 Tickets. Zum Jubiläum „70 Jahre Porsche Sportwagen" im Jahr 2018 wechselte das Event in die Stuttgarter Porsche Arena. Dort konnten nicht nur 3.500 Tickets angeboten, sondern auch ein neues und dynamischeres Konzept von STAGG & FRIENDS realisiert werden. Das Ergebnis war ein lautstarker Abend mit 13 seltenen, historischen und aktuellen Motorsportfahrzeugen sowie 16 Porsche-Motorsportlegenden.

DIE „PORSCHE SOUND NACHT" INSZENIERT 13 SPORTWAGEN UND 16 MOTORSPORT-LEGENDEN ALS DYNAMISCHE SHOW.

THE "PORSCHE SOUND NIGHT" SETS THE SCENE FOR 13 SPORTS CARS AND 16 MOTORSPORTS LEGENDS AS A DYNAMIC SHOW.

The "Porsche Sound Night" has already taken place seven times in Stuttgart, up until now at the Porsche Museum on a little stage, without driving activities and with 911 tickets. For the anniversary "70 Years Porsche Sports Car" in the year 2018, the event relocated to the Stuttgart Porsche Arena, where it was not only possible to offer 3500 tickets but also to realise a new and more dynamic concept by STAGG & FRIENDS. The result was a loud evening with 13 rare, historical and current motorsports vehicles, as well as 16 Porsche motorsports legends.

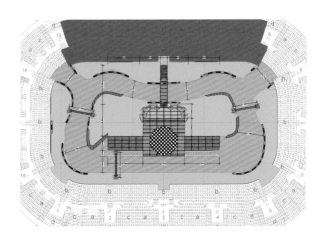

Die zentrale Veranstaltungsfläche wurde zur Rennstrecke und Bühne, die sowohl Porsche-Zeitzeugen als auch die Fahrzeuge gemeinsam in Szene setzte. So konnten die Besucher die fahrenden Sportwagen von allen Seiten sehen und hören. Eine Soundinszenierung mit Songs der letzten 70 Jahre eröffnete die Show. Fünf Performancekünstler im Rennsportoutfit erzeugten mithilfe von Vibrationssensoren präzise Trommel- und Wischbewegungen auf einem Porsche Panamera und somit den Rhythmus zur Soundcollage. Jedes im Anschluss einfahrende Auto wurde von Zeitzeugen wie Jacky Ickx, Derek Bell und Hans-Joachim Stuck mit ganz persönlichen Erlebnissen präsentiert. Emotionale Medieneinspieler aus der Motorsportgeschichte untermalten die Show auf dem zentralen Videowürfel; digitale Bandenelemente entlang der Rennstrecke dienten der Informationsvermittlung. Höhepunkt jedes Auftritts war die pure Motorsoundpräsentation auf einer zentralen Drehscheibe.

The central event area became a racetrack and a stage that set the scene for both the contemporary Porsche witnesses and the vehicles. The visitors could see and hear the driving sportscars from all sides. A sound feature with songs from the last 70 years opened the show. Five performance artists in racing sport outfits created precise drumming and wiping movements on a Porsche Panamera with the help of vibration sensors, providing the rhythm for the sound collage. Each car subsequently driving in was presented by contemporary witnesses such as Jacky Ickx, Derek Bell and Hans-Joachim Stuck with their own personal experiences. Emotional media inserts from motorsports history accompanied the show on the central video cube. Digital strip elements along the racetrack served the purpose of conveying information. The highlight of each performance was the pure motor sound presentation on a central turntable.

SOMMER AM U
PLEASE DON'T TOUCH GBR, DORTMUND

Location
Dortmunder U Courtyard

Client
Dortmunder U, Zentrum für Kunst und
Kreativität, Dortmund

Month / Year
June – July 2018

Duration
2 months

Direction / Coordination
Dortmunder U (André Becker); Heimatdesign (Marc Röbbecke, Reinhild Kuhn)

Architecture / Design
please don't touch GbR, Dortmund

Graphics / Media
konter – Studio für Gestaltung, Dortmund

Lighting
Fachtechnischer Dienst Dortmunder U

Music
Adam Kroll (Sound composition)

Artists / Show acts
See website: sommer-am-u.de/2018

Realisation
please don't touch GbR (Alicja Jelen,
Clemens Müller), Dortmund; Fachtechnischer Dienst Dortmunder U (Uwe Gorski)

Others
Stephan Karass (Metal construction)

Photos
Clemens Müller, please don't touch GbR,
Dortmund

EIN FUTURISTISCH GESTALTETER VOR-PLATZ INSZENIERT EINE KULTUR-VERANSTALTUNG ALS POSTMODERNE VISION.

Seit 2014 findet jährlich der „Sommer am U" statt. Eine Veranstaltungsreihe, die über zwei Monate hinweg unter anderem zu Konzerten, Lesungen und Poetry-Slams einlädt. Jeden Donnerstag und Sonntag können Interessierte zum Vorplatz des Dortmunder U kommen, zuhören oder mitmachen. Der Eintritt ist frei. Mittlerweile hat sich das vom Dortmunder U und Heimatdesign initiierte Event zu einer festen Größe in der städtischen Kulturlandschaft entwickelt – und sollte im fünften Jahr mit einem neuen Look überraschen.

The "Sommer am U" (Summer at the U) has been held every year since 2014. It is an event series that invites visitors to concerts, readings and poetry slams, amongst other things, over the course of two months. Every Thursday and Sunday, those interested can come to the forecourt of the Dortmund U to listen or participate. Entry is free. In the meantime, the event initiated by the Dortmund U and Heimatdesign has developed into a fixed feature in the metropolitan cultural landscape – and was to surprise with a new look in its fifth year.

A FUTURISTICALLY DESIGNED FORECOURT SETS THE SCENE FOR A CULTURAL EVENT AS A POSTMODERN VISION.

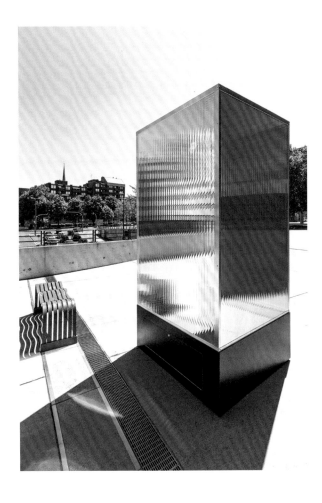

The scenography studio please don't touch developed a contrasting concept that went consciously against the previous forecourt design. The pallet garden formerly planted with greenery was transformed into a futuristic design reminiscent of science fiction films such as *Blade Runner*, *Tron* and *Ghost in the Shell*. Cubes covered with a dichroic film generated glittering light effects and told of a postmodern vision. A matt black container formed the closable stage. Modest stands served as seating for the visitors. An electronic sound composed especially opened and concluded each event.

Das Szenografie-Studio please don´t touch entwickelte ein kontrastierendes Konzept, das der vorherigen Vorplatzgestaltung bewusst entgegenstand. Der ehemals grünbepflanzte Palettengarten verwandelte sich in ein futuristisches Design, das an Science-Fiction-Filme wie *Blade Runner*, *Tron* und *Ghost in the Shell* erinnert. Kuben, die mit dichroider Folie bezogen wurden, erzeugen schillernde Lichteffekte und erzählen von einer postmodernen Vision. Ein mattschwarzer Container bildet die verschließbare Bühne. Schlichte Tribünen dienen den Besuchern als Sitzgelegenheit. Ein eigens komponierter elektronischer Sound eröffnet und schließt jede Veranstaltung.

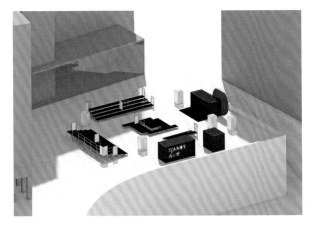

ZAUBERWALD LENZERHEIDE – FASZINATION FÜR ALLE SINNE
VEREIN ZAUBERWALD LENZERHEIDE

Location
Eichhörnchenwald Lenzerheide

Client
Verein Zauberwald Lenzerheide,
Lenzerheide

Month / Year
December 2018

Duration
16 days

Direction / Coordination / Design
Verein Zauberwald Lenzerheide:
Claudia Züllig, Andrea Pallioppi,
Giancarlo Pallioppi, Primo Berera

Curation / Lighting
Kunst- und Designkollektiv NOA:
Primo Berera, Mika Schell

Graphics
PRIMOCOLLECTIVE AG, Lantsch/Lenz:
Primo Berera, Stephan Koritsch

Realisation / Production / Winter Village
Zauberwald Lenzerheide:
Elias Meier

Music / Artists / Show acts
Verein Zauberwald Lenzerheide:
Giancarlo Pallioppi; Martin Koch,
Fettes Haus

Photos
Cemil Erkoc, Johannes Fredheim,
Stephan Koritsch

Internet
www.zauberwald-lenzerheide.ch

Lichtfestivals haben sich zu einem der beliebtesten Formate unter den öffentlichen Events entwickelt. Fast jede größere Stadt bietet in den dunklen Monaten ein Programm aus Licht und Kunst, um die Region mit Unterhaltungsangeboten zu stärken. Doch darunter gibt es besonders innovative Veranstaltungskonzepte, die sich von der Masse abheben. Der Zauberwald in der Lenzerheide ist so ein Event. Es findet seit 2013 jährlich in der Vorweihnachtszeit statt und war das erste Weihnachtsfestival seiner Art in der Schweiz. Inmitten der Natur und unter freiem Himmel begeistern Lichtkunst, Livemusik und einheimische kulinarische Köstlichkeiten die Besucher. Realisiert wird das „Festival für alle Sinne" vom Verein Zauberwald Lenzerheide und genießt mittlerweile eine Beliebtheit bis weit über die Schweizer Landesgrenze hinaus.

EIN UNKONVEN-TIONELLES WEIHNACHTS-EVENT AUS LICHTKUNST, LIVEMUSIK UND KULINARIK INMITTEN DER NATUR UND UNTER FREIEM HIMMEL.

Light festivals have become one of the most popular formats among public events. Almost every major city offers a programme of light and art during the dark months to promote the region with entertainment features. However, among them there are event concepts that particurlarly stand out from the masses for their innovation. The Magic Forest in the Lenzerheide is one such event. It has taken place annually since 2013 in the pre-Christmas period and was the first Christmas festival of its kind in Switzerland. Amidst nature and under an open sky artistic works of light, live music and local culinary treats have been enthusing visitors. The „Festival for All Senses" is realised by the Verein Zauberwald Lenzerheide and by now has achieved a popularity far beyond the Swiss border.

AN UNCONVENTIONAL CHRISTMAS EVENT OF LIGHT ART, LIVE MUSIC AND CUISINE AT THE HEART OF NATURE AND UNDER AN OPEN SKY.

Unter der Kuration des Kunst- und Designkollektivs NOA führt ein mit Lichtinstallationen inszenierter Rundgang durch den dorfnah gelegenen Eichhörnchenwald. Wechselnde nationale und internationale Illuminationskünstler verwandeln den Wald alljährlich in ein unkonventionelles Sinnesfestival. Am Ende des Weges gelangen die Besucher in das Marktdörfchen, wo der Zauberwald gastronomische Angebote in gemütlicher Atmosphäre bietet. Kinderprogramme sowie tägliche Livekonzerte gestalten eine abwechslungsreiche Reihe von Veranstaltungen über knapp zweieinhalb Wochen. 10 % des Eventbudgets werden jährlich ins Marketing investiert. Die eigene Website ist Dreh- und Angelpunkt aller Aktivitäten rund um Print, Online und Social Media.

Curated by the art and design collective NOA, a circuit animated by light installations leads through the forest near the village. Varying national and international illumination artists transform the forest every year into an unconventional feast for the senses. At the end of the walk, visitors reach the little market village where the Magic Forest offers gastronomic options in a leisurely atmosphere. Children's programmes and daily live concerts present a varied spectrum of events over around two weeks. 10 % of the event budget is invested into marketing every year. The dedicated website is the hub of all activities surrounding print, online and social media.

DONA NOBIS PACEM
WESTERMANN KULTURPROJEKTE, INGELHEIM

Location
South façade of Cologne Cathedral

Client
Metropolitan Kapitel der Hohen Domkirche
zu Köln, Cologne

Month / Year
September 2018

Duration
several days

Awards
Deutscher Lichtdesign-Preis 2019

Direction / Coordination
Westermann Kulturprojekte, Ingelheim

Media
Lang Medientechnik, Mannheim

Music
Kölner Domchor, Gürzenich-Orchesters
Köln, figuralchor Köln / Ensemble Harmonia

Artists
Bewegtbild-Projektion, Detlef Hartung &
Georg Trenz, Cologne / Munich

Sound
Live Production, Cologne

Photos
Hartung/Trenz

Im September 2018 wurde zum ersten Mal in der Geschichte des Kölner Doms eine thematische Lichtinszenierung auf der Außenfassade zugelassen und realisiert. Westermann Kulturprojekte entwickelte im Auftrag des Domkapitels der Hohen Domkirche zu Köln eine Inszenierung, die die Erinnerung an den Ersten Weltkrieg mit dem aktuellen Thema des gesellschaftlichen Zusammenhalts verbinden sollte. Der Kölner Dom sollte ein „Leuchtturm des Friedens" sein und alle Menschen einladen, die zum Frieden beitragen möchten. Das Ergebnis war eine gefühlvolle Inszenierung, die sowohl die Fassade des Kölner Doms als auch den Roncalliplatz einband.

DER KÖLNER DOM WIRD MITHILFE EINER EMOTIONALEN LICHTINSZENIERUNG ZUM „LEUCHTTURM DES FRIEDENS".

COLOGNE CATHEDRAL BECOMES A "BEACON OF PEACE" BY MEANS OF AN EMOTIONAL PLAY OF LIGHT.

In September 2018, a themed light show on the external façade of Cologne Cathedral was permitted and realised for the first time in its history. Westermann Cultural Projects developed a scenography, on appointment by the Metropolitan Chapter of Cologne Cathedral, that was to combine a reminder of the First World War with the current topic of social cohesion. Cologne Cathedral was to be a "beacon of peace" and invite all people who wish to contribute to peace. The result was an emotive staging that incorporated both the façade of Cologne Cathedral and Roncalliplatz.

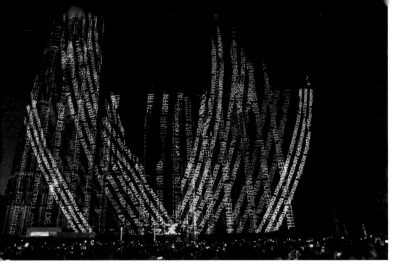

Die Gestaltung der Fassadenprojektion übernahmen die Medienkünstler Detlef Hartung und Georg Trenz, die ausschließlich mit bewegter Typografie arbeiten. Für die Kölner Lichtinszenierung fanden sie ausgehend von den Schock-Erfahrungen des Ersten Weltkriegs Wortbilder für die Sehnsucht nach Frieden. Die Bewegtbild-Projektion reichte bis zur Turmspitze in 157 Meter Höhe und zog sich über die komplette Breite. Musikalisch untermalt wurde sie durch Auszüge aus dem Requiem von Luigi Cherubini und der h-Moll-Messe von J. S. Bach. Wortskulpturen auf dem Roncalliplatz griffen das Thema Frieden in zwölf verschiedenen Sprachen auf. Als Ablageort für Friedenslichter sollten sie die Projektion ergänzen und für die Besucher erfahrbarer machen. So entstand ein atmosphärisches und emotionales Gesamterlebnis aus projizierten und natürlichen Lichtern, das in fünf Tagen knapp 150.000 Menschen anzog. Besondere technische Herausforderungen waren nicht nur die Größe der Projektion, sondern auch die unterschiedlichen Gesteinsmaterialien sowie großen Abstände zwischen dem Strebewerk und der eigentlichen Fassade des Kirchenschiffs.

The design of the façade projection was taken on by the media artists Detlef Hartung and Georg Trenz, who work exclusively with moving typography. For the Cologne light show, they found word pictures for the yearning for peace, based on the shock experiences of the First World War. The moving image projection reached as far as the spire at a height of 157 metres and spanned its entire width. It was accompanied musically by extracts from the Requiem by Luigi Cherubini and the Mass in B Minor by J. S. Bach. Word sculptures on the square Roncalliplatz took up the theme of peace in twelve different languages. As a gathering place for peace lights, they were intended to supplement the projection and enhance the experience for the visitors. This resulted in an atmospheric and emotional overall experience comprising projected and natural lights, which drew around 150,000 people over five days. Special technical challenges were presented not only by the scale of the projection but also the different stone materials and large gaps between the buttresses and the actual façade of the church nave.

Jede Zielgruppe hat unterschiedliche Bedürfnisse und Erwartungen. Dementsprechend sind Eventkonzepte im Idealfall nicht nur auf den Absender, sondern vor allem auf die Empfänger zugeschnitten.

CONSUMERS: VERBRAUCHER ODER KONSUMENTEN, DIE EINE ODER MEHRERE WAREN ODER DIENSTLEISTUNGEN ZUR EIGENEN (PRIVATEN) BEDÜRFNISBEFRIEDIGUNG KÄUFLICH ERWERBEN WOLLEN ODER VIELMEHR SOLLEN. DABEI HANDELT ES SICH MEIST UM NOCH UNBEKANNTE, ABER SCHON INTERESSIERTE PERSONEN, DIE ZU LANGJÄHRIGEN, TREUEN KUNDEN WERDEN KÖNNTEN UND DAMIT DER ABSATZFÖRDERUNG VON UNTERNEHMEN DIENEN.

Each target group has different requirements and expectations. Event concepts are therefore ideally not only geared towards the addressor, but especially towards the recipients.

CONSUMERS: CONSUMERS OR USERS ARE THOSE WHO WANT TO OR SHOULD PURCHASE ONE OR SEVERAL PRODUCTS OR SERVICES TO SATISFY THEIR OWN (PRIVATE) REQUIREMENTS. THEY ARE MOSTLY STILL UNKNOWN, BUT ALREADY INTERESTED PERSONS WHO COULD BECOME LONG-STANDING, LOYAL CUSTOMERS AND THEREFORE BENEFIT THE SALES PROMOTION OF THE COMPANY.

INTERPRINT INTERIOR FESTIVAL – HUB
DIIIP, COLOGNE

Location
Zeche Zollverein SANAA-Gebäude, Essen

Client
Interprint GmbH, Arnsberg

Month / Year
November 2018

Duration
2 days

Direction / Coordination
Interprint GmbH, Arnsberg; Diiip Projekt
GmbH, Cologne

Architecture / Design
Diiip Projekt GmbH, Cologne

Lighting
B&L Eventtec, Ratingen

Film
WITJA Filmproduktion, Hamburg

Music
DJ Fangkiebassbeton (Dirk Kels), Cologne

Speakers
Prof. Timo Rieke (HAWK Hildesheim);
Raphael Gielgen (Vitra GmbH); Antonia
Schmitz (Craftfair); Prof. Dipl. Ing. Sabine
Keggenhoff (Keggenhoff Partner); Massimo
Iosa Ghini (Iosa Ghini Associati); Barbara
Busse (Future + You); Elisabetta Rizzato
(Italianbark); Interprint Design Team
(Salvatore Figliuzzi, Maurizio Burrato,
Daniel Heitkamm)

Catering
Genussarchitekten, Essen

Realisation
Heinemann Möbel-Objekt-Design GmbH,
Bad Driburg; Diiip Projekt GmbH, Cologne

Photos
Thorsten Arendt Fotografie, Münster

EIN INTER-DISZIPLINÄRES MARKETINGEVENT INFORMIERT UND INSPIRIERT ÜBER DAS EIGENE PRODUKT HINAUS.

Kunden oder Partner zu einer einfachen Produktvorstellung mit Häppchen einzuladen, bringt heute nur wenig. Sofern die Gäste überhaupt kommen, wird das Gesehene wohl nicht lange in Erinnerung bleiben. Ein zeitgemäßes Lockmittel sind dagegen Mehrwerte, die über das eigene Produkt hinausgehen. Ein Beispiel dafür ist das Interprint Interior Festival, das von DIIIP entwickelt und realisiert wurde. Als Produzent von Oberflächendekoren lud das Unternehmen 600 Gäste zu einem interdisziplinären Event ein, das informieren und inspirieren sollte.

Inviting customers or partners to a simple product presentation with canapés achieves little nowadays. If the guests come at all, what has been seen will not be remembered for long. Added values that go beyond the product itself, on the other hand, are a contemporary enticement. An example of this is the Interprint Interior Festival that was developed and realised by DIIIP. As a producer of surface decors, the company invited 600 guests to an interdisciplinary event designed to inform and inspire.

AN INTER-DISCIPLINARY MARKETING EVENT INFORMS AND INSPIRES BEYOND THE PRODUCT ITSELF.

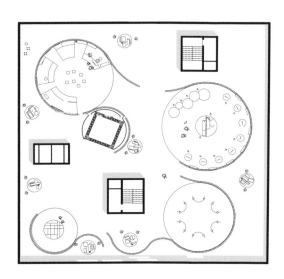

In den Räumlichkeiten des SANAA-Gebäudes auf dem
Unesco-Welterbe Zollverein in Essen entstand eine Mi-
schung aus informativem Speakerevent und selbstexplorati-
ver Dekorausstellung. Im Erdgeschoss kamen internationale
Designer, Architekten, Blogger, Trend- und Zukunftsfor-
scher zu Wort. Hier fanden auch das Catering, die Lounge
und Partner ihren Platz, die zum Networking beitragen sollten. Das Obergeschoss widmete sich den Themen Dekore,
Trends, Farben und Maker. Eingebettet in Palisadenwände
aus Druckerhülsen inszenierten kreisförmige Ausstellungs-
podeste die jeweiligen Themenschwerpunkte. Inhaltlich
fokussierte sich die Ausstellung auf einzelne, erfolgreiche
Designtrends, anstatt mit einer großen Auswahl zu über-
fordern. Zudem wurden alle Themenbereiche selbstexplo-
rativ konzipiert, sodass Besucher Materialien und Trends
möglichst selbst erforschen, erleben und zum Beispiel in
der Maker-Area auch selbst gestalten konnten. Mithilfe von
live geschnittenen Besucherkurzfilmen, einer Microsite,
Instagram und diversen Fachzeitschriften wurde das Event
medial verbreitet.

A mix of informative speaker event and self-explorative
décor exhibition was created on the premises of the SANAA
building on the UNESCO world heritage site Zollverein in
Essen. International designers, architects, bloggers, trend
and future researchers held talks on the ground floor. The
catering, lounge and partners were also accommodated
here with the idea of contributing to networking. The upper
floor was dedicated to the themes of décor, trends, colours
and makers. Embedded among stakewalls made of printer
cartridges, circular exhibition platforms staged the respective thematic focal points. In terms of content, the exhibition
focused on individual successful design trends instead of
an overwhelming wide selection. In addition, all the themes
had a self-explorative conception so that visitors could
discover and experience materials and trends themselves
as far as possible and even for example work with them in
the maker area. With the help of short visitor films cut live,
a microsite, Instagram and various specialist magazines, the
event was broadcast in the media.

LAUNCH OF THE NEW LAMBORGHINI URUS
DEPARTÁMENT, MOSCOW

Location
Moscow Museum, Moscow

Client
Automobili Lamborghini S.p.A., Sant'Agata Bolognese

Month / Year
February 2018

Duration
1 day

Production
Petr Ivanov, Pavel Nedostoev, Yulia Sigunova

Direction / Coordination / Design / Lighting / Media
DEPARTÁMENT, Moscow: Alexander Millin (Direction); Maxim Meshkov (Coordination); Maria Mitsuo, Maxim Yanovskiy, Danila Kuchumov (Design); Stepan Novikov (Lighting)

Show concept & design
Sila Sveta

Music
Monoleak Sound Design, Moscow; Koloah; Ohota

Construction
Max Group, Moscow

Photos
Andrey Buzin

Am 15. Februar 2018 fand in Moskau die große Premiere des Lamborghini Urus, des ersten Super-SUV der Welt, statt. Entsprechend aufsehenerregend sollte die Präsentation des Wagens sein. Die Agentur DEPARTÁMENT entwickelte eine komplexe Bühnenshow mit effektvollem Einsatz von Projection Mapping, 14 Projektoren mit 4-K-Auflösung, diversen Multimedia-Technologien und 56 kinetischen Objekten. In Kombination mit der Raumtiefe und der bewussten Berücksichtigung von Perspektiven und Blickwinkeln entstand eine außergewöhnliche Präsentation.

EINE TECHNISCH AUSGEFEILTE UND RÄUMLICH RAFFINIERTE PRÄSENTATION DES ERSTEN SUPER-SUV.

Die technologische Hauptinnovation der Bühnenshow war ein speziell entwickelter Software-Algorithmus, der die Bewegungen aller 56 kinetischen Dreiecke berechnete. Die visuellen und künstlerischen Inhalte wurden auf diese Weise nahtlos mit dem technischen Teil verbunden, sodass alle beteiligten Oberflächen – kinetische Objekte, Betonsäulen und eine Leinwand im Hintergrund – ein eindrucksvolles, stimmiges Gesamtbild boten.

On 15 February 2018, the major premiere of the Lamborghini Urus, the first super SUV in the world, took place in Moscow. The vehicle's presentation was designed to be suitably spectacular. The agency DEPARTÁMENT developed a complex stage show with an effective use of projection mapping, 14 4-K-resolution projectors, various multimedia technologies and 56 kinetic objects. In combination with the spatial depth and a conscious consideration of perspectives and viewing angles, the result was an exceptional presentation.

A TECHNICALLY POLISHED AND SPATIALLY INGENIOUS PRESENTATION OF THE FIRST SUPER SUV.

The main technological innovation of the stage show was a specially developed software algorithm that calculated the movements of all 56 kinetic triangles. The visual and artistic content was thus combined seamlessly with the technical components so that all the involved surfaces – kinetic objects, concrete columns and a screen in the background – provided an impressive and atmospheric overall image.

RE:IMAGINE STREET ART
CHEIL GERMANY GMBH, SCHWALBACH

Location
ART Berlin 2018, Berlin

Client
Samsung Electronics Germany GmbH,
Schwalbach

Month / Year
September 2018

Duration
several days

Awards
Gold at BrandEx, Bronze at Eurobest,
Gold + Bronze at Deutscher Digital Award,
Winner Webby Award

Others
XI Design, Berlin; Lux von Morgen,
Hamburg; Artificial Rome, Berlin; VR Nerds,
Hamburg

Photos
Cheil Germany GmbH, Schwalbach

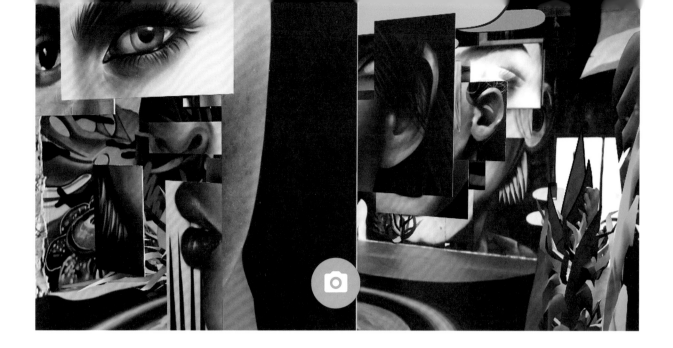

EINE AR-APP, DURCH DIE ANALOGE UND DIGITALE KUNST MITEINANDER VERSCHMELZEN.

Eingebettet in das Kunstfestival Art Berlin 2018 realisierten Samsung und Cheil Germany ein Projekt, das analoge und digitale Kunst miteinander verband. Gemeinsam mit fünf internationalen Künstlern entstanden Kunstwerke in eigenen Pop-up-Galerien, an Wänden und Denkmälern. Jedes Werk beschäftigte sich mit einem ausgewählten Thema, das sich in Skulpturen, Collagen oder einer Fusion aus gegensätzlichen Elementen widerspiegelte. Die Besonderheit war eine Augmented-Reality-App, die die Kunstwerke um eine zusätzliche, digitale Ausdrucks- und Erlebnisebene erweiterte.

Embedded in the context of the art festival Art Berlin 2018, Samsung and Cheil Germany realised a project which combined analogue and digital art. Together with five international artists, works of art were created in their own pop-up galleries, on walls and monuments. Each art piece reflected a selected theme in sculptures, collages or a fusion of contrasting elements. A special feature was an Augmented Reality app which extended the works of art with an additional digital level of expression and experience.

AN AR APP THAT MERGES ANALOGUE AND DIGITAL ART INTO ONE.

Die teilnehmenden Künstler hatten die Möglichkeit, ihre Ideen auf digitaler Ebene weiterzudenken. So kreierten sie lebendige Murals verteilt über ganz Berlin, versetzten Denkmäler in eine virtuelle Welt und spielten im Boros Bunker mit Kunstwerken und Wahrnehmungsebenen. Besucher konnten wiederum mithilfe der Augmented-Reality-App in eine digitale und teilweise interaktive Erweiterung der Kunstwerke eintauchen. Die App diente den Besuchern gleichzeitig als Führer zu den zwölf Locations und öffentlichen Plätzen. Eine dazugehörige Website informierte Besucher und Interessierte über die Werke, Künstler und Entstehungsphasen.

The participating artists had the opportunity to add a new digital layer to their artworks. Spread throughout Berlin, their creations included animated murals, monuments that were transposed into a virtual world and art at the Boros Collection, playing with levels of perception. Visitors, in turn, could immerse themselves in a digital and partly interactive extension of the works of art by means of the Augmented Reality app. At the same time, the app served as a visitors' guide to the twelve locations and public areas. An accompanying website informed visitors and those interested about works, artists and stages of development.

Jede Zielgruppe hat unterschiedliche Bedürfnisse und Erwartungen. Dementsprechend sind Eventkonzepte im Idealfall nicht nur auf den Absender, sondern vor allem auf die Empfänger zugeschnitten.

PARTNERS: VERBUNDENE UNTERNEHMEN, (ZWISCHEN-) HÄNDLER ODER VERTRIEBS- PARTNER, DEREN INFORMA- TIONSHINTERGRUND BEREITS AUF EINE EBENE GEBRACHT WURDE ODER NUN GEBRACHT WERDEN SOLL. DEMENT- SPRECHEND HOMOGEN IST DIESE ZIELGRUPPE ZUSAMMEN- GESTELLT, DEREN ANSPRACHE DIREKT UND EXTREM ZIEL- ORIENTIERT GEHANDHABT WERDEN KANN.

Each target group has different requirements and expectations. Event concepts are therefore ideally not only geared towards the addressor, but especially towards the recipients.

PARTNERS: THESE ARE ASSOCIATED COMPANIES, (INTERMEDIARY) DISTRIBUTORS OR SALES PARTNERS WHO ALREADY HAVE A CERTAIN LEVEL OF BACKGROUND INFORMATION, OR FOR WHOM THIS IS NOW TO BE PROVIDED. THIS TARGET GROUP THEREFORE HAS A HOMOGENEOUS COMPOSITION AND CAN BE APPEALED TO DIRECTLY AND IN A VERY TARGET-ORIENTATED MANNER.

AUDI DEALER MEETING VIENNA 2018
SCHMIDHUBER, MUNICH; MUTABOR, HAMBURG

Location
Marxhalle / Trambahnmuseum, Vienna;
Driving Camp Pachfurth

Client
AUDI AG, Ingolstadt

Month / Year
June 2018

Duration
20 days (2 days per event)

Concept / Architecture
SCHMIDHUBER, Munich

Concept / Product show / Film / Music
MUTABOR, Hamburg

Graphics
DESIGNLIGA, Munich

Lighting
FOUR TO ONE LIGHTING DESIGN GmbH,
Bornheim

Media
TFN GmbH & Co. KG, Hamburg

Decoration
SCHMIDHUBER, Munich; marbet GmbH &
Co. KG, Künzelsau

Catering
Kofler Company AG, Munich

Realisation
A&A Expo International; MT Wijk bij
Durstede, NL

Photos
Stefan Bösl, Ingolstadt

INTENSIVE PRODUKTERLEBNISSE UND EINBLICKE IN DIE ENTWICKLUNG SOLLEN DIE MARKENBINDUNG STÄRKEN.

At the Audi Dealer Meeting 2018, dealers and importers were to be given ample opportunity to experience the products, technology and new vehicles with all their facets. In this, the experience of the guests was a conceptual focus. The three-week event took place in the city of Vienna and at Neusiedler See. Each two-day event started at the Driving Camp Pachfurth at Neusiedler See, where guests could get to know the latest vehicle models A6, Q8 and Audi Sport. Experts were there to offer specialist information and the test track provided an opportunity to try out the driving experience.

Beim Audi Händlermeeting 2018 sollten Händler und Importeure ausreichend Raum erhalten, um die Produkte, Technik und neuen Fahrzeuge in all ihren Facetten zu erleben. Dabei stand das Erlebnis der Gäste im konzeptionellen Mittelpunkt. Veranstaltungsorte für das dreiwöchige Event waren die Stadt Wien und der Neusiedler See. Im Driving Camp Pachfurth am Neusiedler See begann die jeweils zweitägige Veranstaltung. Dort konnten die Gäste die neuesten Fahrzeugmodelle A6, Q8 und Audi Sport kennenlernen. Experten boten Fachinformationen und die Teststrecke eine Gelegenheit, das Fahrvergnügen auszukosten.

Für das anschließende Galadiner bestiegen die Teilnehmer eine historische Tram mit dem Ziel Wiener Tramwaymuseum. Die Raumgestaltung griff die Gebäudearchitektur auf und setzte sie als Neuinterpretation der Wiener Klassik um. Tradition und Innovation sollten sinnbildlich die Werte der Marke kommunizieren. Der zweite Tag stellte die Händler als „Macher" ins Zentrum. Der Makers Space war Ort für Austausch zwischen Gästen und Audi-Mitarbeitern. Die spektakuläre Produktshow im Makers Club drehte schließlich die klassische Inszenierung um, sodass der Zuschauer selbst zum Mittelpunkt des Geschehens wurde.

INTENSIVE PRODUCT EXPERIENCES AND INSIGHTS INTO DEVELOPMENT ARE DESIGNED TO STRENGTHEN BRAND LOYALTY.

For the follow-up gala dinner, the participants boarded a historical tram heading for the the Vienna Tramway Museum. Its spatial design took up the architecture of the building and presented it as a reinterpretation of Viennese classicism. Tradition and innovation were intended to communicate the values of the brand symbolically. The second day was to put a focus on the traders as "makers". The Makers Space was a place for guests and Audi employees to have lively discussions. A spectacular product show at the Makers Club finally reversed classical staging, making the spectator himself the focus of the story.

MERCEDES-BENZ SERVICEGIPFEL #SG10
MILLA & PARTNER, STUTTGART

Location
Flughafen Tempelhof, Berlin

Client
Daimler AG / Mercedes-Benz Vertrieb
Deutschland, Berlin

Month / Year
June 2018

Duration
3 days

**Dramaturgy / Direction / Coordination /
Architecture / Design / Graphics**
Milla & Partner, Stuttgart

Lighting / Media
Production Office, Berlin (Technische Fach-
planung); Production Resource Group AG,
Frankfurt am Main (Technische Umsetzung)

Decoration
Milla & Partner, Stuttgart (Planung);
Party Rent Group, Berlin (Ausführung)

Realisation
kubix Gesellschaft mbH, Berlin

Photos
Offenblende.de – Agentur für Fotografie,
Berlin

EIN OFFENES FORMAT MIT MARKANTEM RAUMDESIGN MACHT DIE DIGITALISIERUNG UND IHRE ENTWICKLUNGEN SICHTBAR.

In 2018, the Service Summit was held for the first time in Berlin by Mercedes-Benz Sales Germany as an internal event series. Milla & Partner created a new dialogue platform at the former Tempelhof airport. The event format along with the design and procedures were completely newly thought out and offered a wide range of information and experiences spanning several thousand square metres. 11,500 visitors and around 200 internal and external exhibitors were part of a three-day exhibition with evening events.

2018 fand der ServiceGipfel als interne Eventreihe des Mercedes-Benz Vertriebs Deutschland erstmalig in Berlin statt. Im ehemaligen Flughafen Tempelhof kreierte Milla & Partner eine neue Dialogplattform. Das Eventformat samt Design und Abläufen wurde komplett neu gedacht und bot ein breites Informations- und Erlebnisangebot auf mehreren Tausend Quadratmetern. 11.500 Besucher und rund 200 interne und externe Aussteller waren Teil einer dreitägigen Ausstellung mit abendlichen Events.

AN OPEN FORMAT WITH A STRIKING SPATIAL DESIGN MAKES DIGITISATION AND ITS DEVELOPMENTS VISIBLE.

Das neue Konzept sah einen deutlichen Bruch zu alten Formaten vor: weg mit Teppichböden und schicken Messeständen, hin zu Rauheit, Improvisation und Offenheit. Ein markantes, reduziertes und offenes Raumdesign schuf eine kommunikative, lockere Atmosphäre. Container in den Hangars 5,6 und 7 dienten als Touchpoints und boten als leuchtend gelbe Objekte Orientierung. Im Zentrum befand sich der offene und wandlungsfähige Campusbereich mit Bühne. Ein eigens für den #SG10 programmiertes Webspecial inklusive Event-App bot Besuchern und Ausstellern größtmöglichen Komfort und Effizienz. Gäste konnten sich vorab über das Programm informieren und ihren Besuch planen. Aussteller hatten die Möglichkeit, ihre Standausstattung aus individuell konfigurierbaren Modulen zusammenzusetzen. So konnten einzelne Bedürfnisse mit einem einheitlichen Erscheinungsbild verbunden werden.

The new concept constituted a clear break with old formats: doing away with carpeted floors and chic trade fair stands in favour or rawness, improvisation and openness. A striking, reduced and open spatial design created a communicative, casual atmosphere. Containers in the hangars 5, 6 and 7 served as touchpoints and provided orientation as brilliant yellow objects. In the centre was the open and flexible campus area with a stage. A specially programmed web special plus app was designed for the #SG10 to offer visitors and exhibitors the greatest possible convenience and efficiency. Guests could find information about the programme in advance and plan their visit. Exhibitors had the possibility to put together their standard model out of modules that could be individually configured. Individual requirements could therefore be combined with a uniform image.

INVESTMENTAKTUELL 2018 – WELTWEITSICHTEN

INSGLÜCK GESELLSCHAFT FÜR MARKEN-INSZENIERUNG MBH, BERLIN

Location
Gesellschaftshaus Palmengarten, Frankfurt am Main

Client
Union Asset Management Holding AG, Frankfurt am Main

Month / Year
May 2018

Duration
1 day

Awards
1 × Silver at BrandEx Awards

Dramaturgy
Detlef Wintzen, insglück, Berlin

Direction / Coordination
Jan Niclas Schatka Erlebnisgestaltung, Bergheim

Lighting
Karsten Krause Lichtdesign, Berlin

Media
Benjamin Sterzenbach, Elberfeld Kreation, Wuppertal

Artists / Show acts
Duo Sonambul; Team Ashigaru; Michael Raivard; Wall Clown; Viktor Kee; Benny & Joyce

Decoration
drei d medien service, Wildau

Others
Marco Franiczek, insglück Cologne (Overall project direction)

Photos
Kaleidomania Axel Gaube, Frankfurt am Main

Die Veranstaltung „InvestmentAktuell" ist ein jährlich statt-
findendes Format der Union Investment. Ihr Ziel ist es, die
mehr als 250 angereisten Gäste und Vorstände aus Partner-
banken über zukunftsweisende Themen zu informieren. So
sollen Begeisterung und Bindung an die Fondsgesellschaft
gestärkt werden. Unter dem Motto „WeltWeitSichten" sollte
der Gastgeber 2018 als vorausschauender Partner inszeniert
werden. Inhaltlich kommunizierte die betreuende Agentur
insglück das Thema „Vorausschauen" als zweigeteilte Eigen-
schaft: bestehend aus einer rational-kognitiven und emo-
tional-intuitiven Komponente. Entsprechend zweigeteilt war
der dramaturgische Aufbau der Veranstaltung.

The event "InvestmentAktuell" is a format held annually by
Union Investment. Its aim is to inform the more than 250
visiting guests and governing bodies of partner banks about
future-orientated themes and to promote enthusiasm and
loyalty to the investment company. Under the motto "World-
WideViews", the host was to be staged as a forward-looking
partner in 2018. In terms of content, the appointed agency
insglück communicated the topic of "Looking ahead" as a
twofold feature: consisting of a rational-cognitive and an
emotional-intuitive component. The dramaturgical structure
of the event was correspondingly twofold.

ZWEI GEGEN- SÄTZLICHE THEMEN WERDEN INHALTLICH SOWIE RÄUMLICH IN EINEM VARIABLEN SETUP INSZENIERT.

Der Fachkongress am Tag widmete sich rational-kognitiven Themen. Vorträge über wirtschaftliche Herausforderungen, nachhaltiges Change Management oder die Funktionsweise des Gedächtnisses standen auf dem Programm. Die Abendgala griff die emotional-intuitive Komponente auf. Eine dreistündige Inszenierung mit Musik, Acts und Mentalmagie beleuchtete verschiedene Kunstepochen. Mit diesem Perspektivwechsel sollten die Schnittstellen des Analytischen und Künstlerischen kommuniziert werden. Ein variables Setup aus einer Vielzahl im Raum verteilter bespielbarer Rahmen ermöglichte es, beide Programmteile räumlich aufzugreifen. Zum Fachkongress wurden Trends, Entwicklungen in der Politik und auf den Finanzmärkten über Grafiken, Diagramme und Weltkarten visualisiert. Abends wurden die Rahmen zu einer sich wandelnden Kunstausstellung durch alle Epochen.

The specialist congress during the day was dedicated to rational-cognitive themes. Presentations about economic challenges, sustainable change management or how memory functions were on the programme. The evening gala took up the emotional-intuitive component. A three-hour staging with music, acts and mental magic illuminated various periods of art. With this shift in perspective, the crossovers between the analytical and artistic were to be communicated. A variable setup with numerous frames distributed around the space that could be animated allowed both parts of the programme to be incorporated spatially. Trends, developments in politics and on the financial markets were visualised by means of graphics, diagrams and world maps at the specialist congress. In the evening, the frames became a varying art exhibition through all eras.

TWO OPPOSING THEMES ARE STAGED IN TERMS OF CONTENT AND SPACE IN A VARIABLE SETUP.

BEST OF BELRON 2018
UNIPLAN GMBH & CO. KG, COLOGNE

Location
Messe Frankfurt

Client
Belron International Ltd, London

Month / Year
June 2018

Duration
2 days

**Dramaturgy / Direction / Coordination /
Architecture / Design / Graphics**
Uniplan GmbH & Co. KG, Cologne

Construction
PRG AG, Cologne

AV & Lighting
Echo-Blanc Culture & Communication Co.,
Ltd., Beijing

Media
Brand New Media, Hamburg

Films
Leitwolf, Hamburg

Music
Nomadstudio, Aachen

Artists / Show acts
New City Beats, Dusseldorf

Decoration
deco event KG, Bad Homburg

Catering
Accente Gastronomie Service GmbH

Others
360GRAD, Hamburg (Technical planning);
Lounge Factory, Hamburg (Furniture);
SpotMe, Lausanne (Event app); InSPE Event
GmbH, Wiesbaden (Driving stunt)

Photos
Robert Schlesinger; Julian Huke;
PRG Production Resource Group AG

EIN WETTBEWERB WÜRDIGT DIE MITARBEITER UND STELLT PARTNERN NEUESTE PRODUKTE IN AKTION VOR.

The event "Best of Belron" in 2018 brought together more than 2000 partners, employees and suppliers in Frankfurt over a period of two days. The subsidiary of Carglass would like to pursue several aims at the same time with this regularly held event. Its purpose is to value their own employees, as well as to introduce partners and suppliers to the latest technologies and tools under real working conditions. At the event in 2018 managed by Uniplan, there was anniversary of the 10th "Best of Belron" in addition.

Das Event „Best of Belron" brachte 2018 über zwei Tage hinweg mehr als 2.000 Partner, Mitarbeiter und Zulieferer in Frankfurt zusammen. Die Tochtergesellschaft von Carglass möchte mit dieser regelmäßig stattfindenden Veranstaltung gleich mehrere Ziele verfolgen. Sie soll die eigenen Mitarbeiter wertschätzen sowie Partnern und Lieferanten die neuesten Technologien und Werkzeuge unter realen Arbeitsbedingungen vorstellen. Bei dem 2018 von Uniplan betreuten Event kam das Jubiläum der 10. „Best of Belron" hinzu.

A COMPETITION VALUES THE EMPLOYEES AND PRESENTS TO THE PARTNERS THE LATEST PRODUCTS IN ACTION.

Das zentrale Konzept versteht sich als eine unkonventionelle
Meisterschaft mit den 30 besten Belron-Autofensterspezialis-
ten der Welt. Dabei wurden vier Wettbewerbe ausgetragen,
bei denen die Teilnehmer ihre Fähigkeiten und ihr Wissen
unter Beweis stellen mussten. Neben einer Konferenz mit
namhaften Rednern, einer Ausstellung mit Marken aus der
Automobilindustrie, einer Preisverleihung sowie einem
Galadiner fanden 2018 mehrere Side-Events mit verschiedenen Dinner-Locations und Aktivitäten statt. Eine Event-App
bot den Besuchern einen Überblick und die Möglichkeit,
eine personalisierte Agenda zu erstellen. Die räumliche
Gestaltung orientierte sich an den typischen Belron-Werk-
stätten: gelbe Bodenmarkierungen, Werkstattleuchten
und Werkbänke. Alle Medien, Grafiken und Bühnenbilder
vereinten das Corporate Design mit einem Meisterschafts-
charakter. Der gesamte Wettbewerb wurde von einem
Reporter begleitet und live übertragen. Ergänzend wurden
Rezensionen, Interviews und Videos produziert und auf
dem YouTube-Markenkanal hochgeladen. Facebook- und
Instagram-Posts hielten das Online-Publikum auf dem
Laufenden.

The central concept is understood as an unconventional
championship with the 30 best Belron car window specialists
in the world. Four competitions were held in which the
participants had to prove their skills and knowledge. Apart
from a conference with renowned speakers, an exhibition
with brands from the automobile industry, a prize award,
a gala dinner and several side events took place in 2018
showcasing various dinner locations and activities. An event
app offered the visitors an overview and the possibility to
put together a personalised agenda. The spatial design
was orientated towards the typical Belron workshops: yellow floor markings, workshop lighting and work benches.
All media, graphics and set designs brought together the
corporate design and a championship character. The whole
competition was accompanied by a reporter and broadcast
live. Reviews, interviews and videos were produced in addition and uploaded onto the YouTube brand channel. Facebook and Instagram posts kept the online public up to date.

Jede Zielgruppe hat unterschiedliche Bedürfnisse und Erwartungen. Dementsprechend sind Eventkonzepte im Idealfall nicht nur auf den Absender, sondern vor allem auf die Empfänger zugeschnitten.

FRIENDS: EIN EXKLUSIVER UND VOR ALLEM AUSGEWÄHLTER KREIS AN GÄSTEN, DER SICH AUS DEN UNTERSCHIEDLICHSTEN ZIELGRUPPEN ZUSAMMENSETZT: PARTNER, KUNDEN, FANS, WEGBEGLEITER, (LOKAL-)PROMINENZ, (BRANCHEN- UND UNTERNEHMENS-)VIPS, EHREN-GÄSTE UND MEDIENVERTRETER. TROTZ KULTURELLER UND GESELLSCHAFTLICHER HETERO-GENITÄT EINT SIE DIE TATSACHE, DASS SIE DEM GASTGEBER FREUNDSCHAFTLICH GESONNEN UND MEIST EINER DIREKTEN EINLADUNG GEFOLGT SIND.

Each target group has different requirements and expectations. Event concepts are therefore ideally not only geared towards the addressor, but especially towards the recipients.

FRIENDS: FRIENDS ARE AN EXCLUSIVE AND SELECTED CIRCLE OF GUESTS COMPOSED OF A WIDE RANGE OF TARGET GROUPS: PARTNERS, CUSTOMERS, FANS, COMPANIONS, (LOCAL) CELEBRITIES, VIPS (FROM COMPANIES AND THE SECTOR), GUESTS OF HONOUR AND MEDIA REPRESENTATIVES. DESPITE CULTURAL AND SOCIAL HETEROGENEITY, THEY ARE UNITED BY THE FACT THAT THEY ARE ON FRIENDLY TERMS WITH THE HOST AND MOSTLY RESPONDED TO A DIRECT INVITATION.

ETIHAD 15 YEAR ANNIVERSARY
FLORA&FAUNAVISIONS GMBH, BERLIN

Location
Louvre, Abu Dhabi

Client
Etihad Airways, Abu Dhabi

Month / Year
October 2018

Duration
1 day

Dramaturgy / Direction / Coordination /
IMG Focus

Architecture / Design
flora&faunavisions GmbH, Berlin;
ABOUTKOKOMO, Berlin

Graphics / Media
flora&faunavisions GmbH, Berlin

Photos
IMG Focus; flora&faunavisions GmbH,
Berlin

2018 feierte Etihad Airways seinen 15. Geburtstag. Das sollte nicht nur mit einem exklusiven und beeindruckenden VIP-Event, sondern auch mit einer neuen Accessoires-Kollektion gefeiert werden. Hierfür hat sich Etihad mit Diane von Fürstenberg zusammengetan und eine limitierte Kollektion entworfen. So standen neben dem Jubiläum auch die neu entwickelten Stoffmuster im inhaltlichen und gestalterischen Fokus der Veranstaltung.

EINE MODE-KOLLEKTION UND IHRE STOFFMUSTER WERDEN ZUM VISUELLEN HIGHLIGHT EINES JUBILÄUMS- UND VIP-EVENTS.

A FASHION COLLECTION AND ITS FABRIC PATTERNS BECOME THE VISUAL HIGHLIGHT OF AN ANNIVERSARY AND VIP EVENT.

In 2018, Etihad Airways celebrated its 15th birthday. This was to be marked not only with an exclusive and impressive VIP event, but also with a new accessories collection. For this purpose, Etihad got together with Diane von Fürstenberg and designed a limited collection. Accordingly, apart from the anniversary, the newly developed fabric patterns were also a content and design focus of the event.

Als Veranstaltungsort suchte man sich den erst 2017 eröffneten Louvre Abu Dhabi mit seiner spektakulären Architektur aus. Die Agenturen IMG Focus, ABOUTKOKOMO und flora&faunavisions machten sich die kubische Architektur von Jean Nouvel zunutze und bespielten sie mit riesigen, nahtlos ineinander übergehenden Projektionen. Inhaltlicher Kern der Projektionen waren die exklusiven Muster der limitierten Kollektion, die nicht nur zur außergewöhnlichen Raumwirkung beitrugen, sondern auf diesem Wege über den Abend hinweg präsent waren.

The choice of event location was the Louvre Abu Dhabi with its spectacular architecture, opened as recently as in 2017. The agencies IMG Focus, ABOUTKOKOMO and flora&faunavisions made use of Jean Nouvel's cubic architecture and animated it with giant projections guided by seamless transitions. The content core of the projections was the exclusive patterns of the limited collection, which not only contributed to the extraordinary spatial effect but in this manner were present throughout the evening.

JOURNEY – 20 JAHRE CEBRA
CEBRA EVENT GMBH, MUNICH

Location
Werk3Studio, Munich

Month / Year
December 2018

Duration
1 day

Dramaturgy / Direction / Coordination
Cebra Event GmbH, Munich

Architecture / Design
Cebra Event GmbH, Munich; dear robinson, Munich

Graphics
dear robinson, Munich

Lighting / Media
Georg Veit Lichtdesign, Munich

Music
Zeno Lechner, Munich; Trio Klezmeron, Nuremberg

Artists / Show acts
Photographer JOURNEY: Urban Zintel, Berlin

Decoration / Realisation
Werk3Studiovermietung GmbH, Munich

Catering
Hackbarths Partyservice OHG, Brunnthal

Photos
Cebra Event GmbH, Munich; Georg Veit, Munich; Marcel Weber, Munich

Kleine, feine, analoge und persönliche Begegnungen sind trotz oder gerade wegen der vorherrschenden Digitalisierung ein gegenläufiger Trend in der Live-Kommunikation. Diesen Ansatz bevorzugte auch die Münchner Event- und Incentive-Agentur Cebra, um ihr 20-jähriges Jubiläum zu feiern. Anstatt sich selbst und eigene Erfolge imposant in Szene zu setzen, entschied man sich, andere Menschen in den Vordergrund zu stellen. Mit analogen und charmanten Geschichten sollte der Agentur-Claim „Unique Stories" zum Leben erweckt werden. In diesem Sinne besuchte Agenturinhaberin Mechthild Banholzer 2018 wichtige Wegbegleiter des Unternehmens. Langjährige Kunden, internationale Partner, Künstler, ehemalige Mitarbeiter, die in insgesamt 9 Ländern zu Hause sind und die Agenturgeschichte mitgeprägt haben. Gemeinsam mit dem Fotografen Urban Zintel entstanden dabei Fotografien und Geschichten, die die Inhalte für das abschließende Jubiläumsevent bildeten.

PERSÖNLICHE BEGEGNUNGEN STATT IMPOSANTER SELBST-INSZENIERUNG – BEWUSST ANALOG UND HARMONISCH GESTALTET.

PERSONAL ENCOUNTERS INSTEAD OF IMPOSING SELF-STAGING – CONSCIOUSLY ANALOGUE AND HARMONIOUSLY DESIGNED.

Small, pleasant, analogue and personal encounters are a reverse trend in live communication despite or precisely because of the predominant digitisation. The Munich event and incentive agency Cebra also preferred this approach to celebrate their 20-year anniversary. Instead of imposingly staging themselves and their successes, they decided to place the focus on other people. With analogous and charming stories, the agency claim of "unique stories" was to be brought to life. In the interests of this, agency owner Mechthild Banholzer visited important persons who accompanied the company along the way. Longstanding customers, international partners, artists, former employees at home in a total of 9 countries and having contributed to the history of the agency. Together with photographer Urban Zintel, this resulted in photographs and stories which formed the content for the concluding anniversary event.

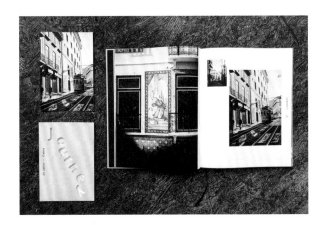

Zentrales Gestaltungselement der Veranstaltung waren 60 ausgewählte Fotografien, die, hochwertig präsentiert, besondere Menschen und Momente feierten. Ein Flying Buffet durch die bereisten Destinationen gab die Reise kulinarisch wieder. Großprojektionen mit weiteren Eindrücken der Reise sowie regionale Klänge, live eingespielt von einem DJ samt Akustik-Trio, unterstützten die jeweils landestypische Atmosphäre. Finale Höhepunkte waren eine Auktion, bei der Fotografien für einen guten Zweck versteigert wurden, und die Vorstellung des Buches *Journey*, eine hochwertige, 160 Seiten starke Hommage an die Wegbegleiter aus 20 Jahren, die jeder Gast als Geschenk erhielt.

The central design element of the event were 60 selected photographs with a high-quality presentation that celebrated special people and moments. A flying buffet through the destinations was a culinary reflection of the journey. Large projections with further impressions of the journey, as well as regional music recorded live by a DJ and an acoustic trio, reinforced the respective typical atmosphere of each country. The final highlights were an auction in which photographs were auctioned for a good cause and the presentation of the book *Journey*, a high-quality, 160-page homage to companions from the last 20 years, given as a gift to each guest.

ABB FIA FORMULA E CHAMPIONSHIP
STANDING OVATION AG, ZURICH

Location
Julius Bär Zürich E-Prix 2018

Client
ABB Asea Brown Boveri Ltd, Zurich

Month / Year
June 2018

Duration
2 days

Dramaturgy
standing ovation ag, Zurich;
heusser.tv gmbh, Zurich

Direction / Coordination / Graphics
standing ovation ag, Zurich

Architecture / Design
Office for spatial identity GmbH, Zurich

Lighting
smARTec Veranstaltungstechnik AG, Aarau;
loop light GmbH, Marburg

Media
Serviceplan One GmbH & Co. KG, Munich;
loop light GmbH, Marburg; BBM Productions
AG, Wallbach

Films
Sebastian Harms

Artists / Show acts
Philipp Fankhauser; Loungejazz; Meute;
High on Heels

Decoration
Expomobilia AG, Illnau-Effretikon;
Richnerstutz AG, Villmergen

Catering
dine & shine Event Catering, Urdorf

Realisation
standing ovation ag, Zurich; Ingenieurbüro
Jens Labuschewski (Crossed Disciplines)

Photos
Selina Meier Fotografie, Zurich

EIN ZENTRALER, PROMINENTER ORT VEREINT VISIBILITÄT, MARKENERLEBNIS UND VERSCHIEDENSTE EVENTS.

Nach 60 Jahren fand 2018 erstmals wieder ein Rundstreckenrennen in der Schweiz statt: die ABB FIA-Formel-E-Meisterschaft. Die Strecke verlief mitten durch Zürich und bot sich ideal für Marketing-Aktivitäten lokaler wie auch globaler Firmen an – wie zum Beispiel für den in Zürich beheimateten Konzern ABB. Erklärtes Ziel war es, während des Julius Bär Zürich E-Prix einen emotional überzeugenden Auftritt zu kreieren. Es sollte ein exklusiver Ort entstehen, der Gala-Atmosphäre und Brand Experience vereinte sowie Platz für verschiedene Eventformate bot.

In 2018, circuit racing returned to Switzerland for the first time in 60 years with the ABB FIA Formula E Championship. The racing series was held on the streets of Zurich, presenting an ideal marketing opportunity for both local companies and global ones, like ABB, which has its headquarters in Zurich. The aim was to create an emotional experience at the Julius Bär Zurich E-Prix with an exclusive event space, designed to bring together a celebratory atmosphere and brand experience, while being versatile enough for a variety of event formats.

A CENTRAL, PROMINENT LOCATION BRINGS TOGETHER VISIBILITY, BRAND EXPERIENCE AND A WIDE VARIETY OF EVENTS.

So entstand in Zusammenarbeit mit standing ovation ein dreistöckiger, weitherum gut sichtbarer Cube direkt über der Start- und Ziellinie der Rennstrecke. Dieser ermöglichte nicht nur von allen Ebenen einen guten Blick auf das Rennen, sondern diente auch als Dinner-Location für 350 Gäste anlässlich des 30-Jahre-Jubiläums der ASEA-/BBC-Fusion. Eine Dachterrasse auf dem 18 Meter hohen Gebäude bot zudem eine hervorragende Aussicht auf den See und die Berge. Die unterschiedlichen Erlebniswelten der einzelnen Ebenen sollten Brand Experience, Race-Erlebnis und das Flair einer Gala mit Konzertbühne und Infotainment auf einen gemeinsamen Nenner bringen sowie gleichzeitig Möglichkeiten schaffen, zu netzwerken und zu entspannen.

In cooperation with standing ovation, a three-storey cube visible from afar was built directly above to the start and finish line of the racing circuit. As well as providing a bird's eye view of the race action from all floors, the cube served as a dinner location for 350 guests to celebrate the 30th anniversary of the ASEA/BBC merger. An 18-metre-high roof terrace also provided stunning views of the lake and mountains. The objective of the unique atmospheres of the individual floors was allowing the guests to experience the race, the brand and a and gala atmosphere with a concert stage for music and infotainment, while having the possibility to network and to relax.

TUI CRUISES CHRISTENING OF THE NEW „MEIN SCHIFF 1"
INSGLÜCK GESELLSCHAFT FÜR MARKEN-INSZENIERUNG MBH, BERLIN

Location
Port of Hamburg

Client
TUI Cruises GmbH, Hamburg

Month / Year
May 2018

Duration
1 day

Awards
1 × Silver and 2 × Bronze at Galaxy Awards

Dramaturgy / Choreography
insglück Hamburg; Eckelmann + Rettig GmbH, Berlin

Lighting
Martin Kuhn Lichtdesign & Produktion, Berlin

Media
flora&faunavisions GmbH, Berlin

Films / Livestream
Sales Cube, Cologne

Music
Robert Henke

Others
Production Resource Group AG, Hamburg (Technics); Production Office POE GmbH, Berlin (Technical Direction); Heiko Hartmann (Costumes, Make-up); Elements Entertainment GmbH, Bielefeld (Fireworks)

Photos
Franziska Krug; Andreas Vallbracht; Christoph Maier

Die Taufe des neuen Mitglieds der Mein-Schiff-Flotte der Hamburger Reederei TUI Cruises – die „Mein Schiff 1" – sollte ein unvergessliches Erlebnis werden. Nicht nur für die 2.500 Gäste an Bord und die 500 Mitarbeiter von TUI Cruises, die im Rahmen eines lockeren Get-togethers von einem Begleitboot aus zuschauten. Eine Kernaufgabe für die betreuende Agentur insglück bestand darin, ein einzigartiges PR-Bild für die Medien zu erzeugen. Um die Besonderheit der Ausstattung hervorzuheben und das erklärte Ziel zu erreichen, entwickelte sie eine royale Leitidee und machte aus der Taufe eine symbolische Krönung.

EINE SCHIFFSTAUFE WIRD ZU EINER SPEKTAKULÄREN KRÖNUNG UND EINEM PR-BILD VOR IMPOSANTER INDUSTRIEKULISSE.

DIE KRÖNUNG DER
Mein Schiff ® FLOTTE

Für diesen Ansatz wurde eine spektakuläre Industriekulisse ausgesucht: Europas zweitgrößter Umschlagplatz für Container, das HHLA Terminal Burchardkai im Hamburger Hafen. Die das Schiff überragenden Kranausleger und Containerbrücken setzten das Taufevent imposant in Szene – und dienten gleichzeitig als Schauplatz einer luftakrobatischen Darbietung im Rahmen der Taufshow mit Tanz-Choreografien. Das 25 Meter lange, komplett mit LEDs überbaute Pooldeck wurde dafür zur virtuellen maritimen Erlebniswelt. Nach der traditionellen Taufe durch das internationale Nummereins-Duo im Beachvolleyball, Kira Walkenhorst und Laura Ludwig, folgte das Finale aus Lichtshow und Feuerwerk. Die fächerförmige Anordnung der Kranausleger sowie üppige Lichtprojektionen und Pyroeffekte bildeten die symbolische Krone – und das beabsichtigte beeindruckende Bild.

The christening of the new member of the Hamburg shipping company TUI Cruises' My Ship fleet – the "My Ship 1" – was to become an unforgettable experience, not only for the 2,500 guests on board and the 500 employees of TUI Cruises watching from a tender as part of a casual get-together. A key task for the appointed agency insglück consisted of generating a unique PR image for the media. To highlight the facilities' special features and to achieve the declared objective, insglück developed a royal guiding idea and turned the christening into a symbolic crowning.

A spectacular industrial setting was selected for this approach: Europe's second largest reloading point for containers, the HHLA Terminal Burchardkai at the Port of Hamburg. The crane jibs and container bridges towering over the ship set an impressive stage for the christening – and served at the same time as the setting of an aerial acrobatics performance in the context of the christening show with its dance choreographies. For this purpose, the 25-metre-long pool deck completely covered with LEDs became a virtual maritime world of experience. After the traditional christening by the international number one pair in beach volleyball, Kira Walkenhorst and Laura Ludwig, a finale comprising a light show and fireworks followed. The fanlike arrangement of the crane jibs and exuberant light projections and pyro effects formed the symbolic crown – and the intended impressive image.

A SHIP CHRISTENING IS TURNED INTO A SPECTACULAR CROWNING AND A PR IMAGE IN FRONT OF AN IMPOSING INDUS-TRIAL BACKDROP.

GAGGENAU RESTAURANT 1683 LA
1ZU33 GMBH, MUNICH

Location
Cooper Building, Los Angeles

Client
Gaggenau Hausgeräte GmbH, Munich

Month / Year
May 2018

Duration
several days

Awards
DDC Gute Gestaltung 2019; Red Dot Award

Dramaturgy / Direction / Coordination /
Architecture / Design
1zu33 GmbH, Munich

Graphics / Lighting / Media / Films /
Music / Artists / Show acts / Decoration
Padre Knows Best, Austin

Catering
Daniel Humm, New York; The NoMad,
New York & LA

Realisation
Altmann Laden- und Innenausbau GmbH,
Bönnigheim

Photos
Roger Davies, New York; Jerritt Clark,
New York

2016 initiierte die Agentur 1zu33 für ihren Kunden Gaggenau eine neue Eventreihe. Die Luxusmarke präsentierte sich und ihre Küchengeräte in einem außergewöhnlich inszenierten Pop-up-Restaurant. Was damals in einer Kunstgalerie in Chelsea New York begann, wurde 2018 in Downtown Los Angeles fortgeführt und leicht weiterentwickelt. Als Anlass diente das 333-jährige Bestehen der Marke. An dem drei-tägigen kulinarischen Event durfte eine limitierte Zahl an Gästen teilnehmen und in einer mystischen Schwarzwald-szenerie die Ursprünge der Firma erleben.

A DETAILED, MYSTICAL SPATIAL DESIGN CREATES AN EXCEPTIONAL BRAND EXPERIENCE AND DINNER EVENT.

EINE DETAILREICHE, MYSTISCHE RAUM-GESTALTUNG SCHAFFT EIN AUSSERGEWÖHN-LICHES MARKEN-ERLEBNIS UND DINNEREVENT.

In 2016, the agency 1zu33 initiated a new event series for their customer Gaggenau. The luxury brand presented itself and its kitchen appliances in an exceptionally staged pop-up restaurant. What started back then in an art gallery in Chelsea New York was continued in 2018 in downtown Los Angeles and developed further somewhat. The 333-year existence of the brand served as an occasion. A limited number of guests were allowed to participate in the three-day culinary event and experience the origins of the company in a mystical Black Forest scene.

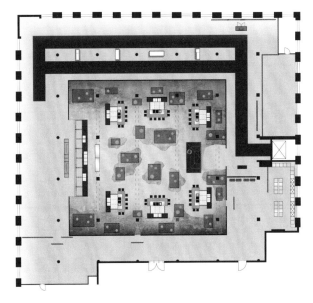

Ein Lastenaufzug brachte die Gäste in den 11. Stock des Cooper Building und empfing sie mit der bereits legendären, übergroßen und stilisierten Kuckucksuhr. Eine Ausstellung bildete den Prolog und präsentierte Exponate, die die Anfänge und Meilensteine des traditionsreichen Unternehmens markierten. Darauf folgte das exklusive Dinnerevent in einer detailverliebt gestalteten Szenerie aus bis zu 6,5 Meter hohen Bäumen, Kunstschnee, Fachwerkelementen und einer mondlichtartigen Beleuchtung. In Anlehnung an die Wurzeln von Gaggenau in der Metallverarbeitung werkte ein Schmied live während der Veranstaltung und sorgte mit kraftvollen metallischen Schlägen für eine akustische Komponente. Der mit drei Michelin-Sternen dekorierte Spitzenkoch Daniel Humm konnte als Küchenchef für die Veranstaltung gewonnen werden. Zusammen mit der Kochcrew bereitete er an sechs mit Gaggenau-Geräten ausgestatteten Stationen live ein Gourmetmenü zu. So entstand erneut ein multisensorisches ganzheitliches Markenerlebnis.

A goods lift took the guests to the 11th floor of the Cooper Building and greeted them with the already legendary, oversized and stylised cuckoo clock. An exhibition formed the prologue and presented exhibits that marked the beginnings and milestones of the traditional enterprise. This was followed by an exclusive dinner event in a setting designed with a love of detail, consisting of trees up to 6.5 metres high, artificial snow, framework elements and illumination like moonlight. In reference to the roots of Gaggenau in metal processing, a smith worked live during the event and provided acoustic components with powerful metallic blows. Top chef Daniel Humm, awarded three Michelin stars, was secured as the chef. Together with the cooking crew, he prepared a gourmet menu at six stations equipped with Gaggenau appliances. This resulted in another multisensory overall brand experience.

A CULINARY EXPEDITION THROUGH DOWNTOWN RIEDEL
ORTVISION, BERLIN

Location
Riedel Communications Headquarters,
Wuppertal

Client
Riedel Communications GmbH & Co. KG

Month / Year
December 2017

Duration
1 day

**Dramaturgy / Direction / Coordination /
Architecture / Design / Graphics / Films**
Riedel Communications GmbH & Co. KG,
Wuppertal / Ortvision, Berlin

Lighting / Media
wige Solutions GmbH & Co. KG,
Meckenheim

Music / Artists / Show acts
Ortvision, Berlin

Decoration
Ortvision, Berlin; Kirberg Catering GmbH,
Cologne

Catering
Kirberg Catering GmbH, Cologne

Photos
Johannes Dreuw Photography, Bonn

DIE WERTE EINER MARKE, INSZENIERT ALS URBANES STADTVIERTEL MIT 14 KULINARISCHEN ERLEBNISRÄUMEN.

The 30th company anniversary of Riedel Communications was celebrated in 2017 with 2000 guests. In the Riedel halls spanning almost 5000 square metres, the company wanted to take their guests with them on a journey. A superior aim was to convey the global and innovative activity of the brand. With this in mind as their concept, Kirberg Catering took up the place where the dynamic diversity of the world presents itself, in the centre of metropolises: downtown. This resulted in the idea of "Downtown Riedel" – a spatial and culinary ramble through 14 space and food concepts.

Das 30. Firmenjubiläum von Riedel Communications wurde 2017 mit 2.000 Gästen gefeiert. In den Riedel-Hallen mit fast 5.000 Quadratmeter Fläche wollte das Unternehmen seine Gäste mit auf eine Reise nehmen. Das übergeordnete Ziel war es, die globale und innovative Aktivität der Marke zu vermitteln. In diesem Sinne griff Kirberg Catering konzeptionell den Ort auf, in dem sich die dynamische Vielfalt der Welt präsentiert, in den Zentren der Metropolen: downtown. So entstand die Idee von „Downtown Riedel" – ein räumlicher sowie kulinarischer Streifzug durch 14 Raum- und Gastrokonzepte.

THE VALUE OF A BRAND, STAGED AS AN URBAN DISTRICT WITH 14 CULINARY WORLDS OF EXPERIENCE.

Mithilfe von Überseecontainern wurde die große Fläche in kleinere Räume, verschiedene Ebenen und Terrassen unterteilt. Das Team entwickelte 14 Bars und Restaurants samt passendem Setting. Die Konzepte orientierten sich an der echten kulinarischen Erlebniswelt, wie man sie in den internationalen Metropolen findet – von einer asiatischen Garküche über Büdchen und Picknick im Park bis zum Butcher. Die Herausforderung bestand darin, die globale Ausrichtung der Marke Riedel über alle Attribute einer Reise zu kommunizieren und ein internationales und eventerfahrendes Publikum zu begeistern. So entstand ein Streifzug durch „Downtown", der Werte und Inhalte der Marke spielerisch erfahrbar machen sollte. Angelehnt an die Empfehlungsplattform „TripAdvisor" bot der „RiedelAdvisor" den Gästen Orientierungsmöglichkeiten. Vertraute Visualisierungen und Beschreibungen zogen sich durch die gesamte Erlebniswelt und machten Lust, auf Entdeckungstour zu gehen.

With the help of overseas containers, the large area was divided into smaller spaces, various levels and terraces. The team developed 14 bars and restaurants along with a suitable setting. The concepts were orientated towards the real culinary world of experience one can find in international metropolises – from an Asian cookshop to little stalls, a picnic in the park and a butcher. The challenge was to communicate Riedel's global orientation as a brand, incorporating all features typically associated with a journey and enthusing an international audience familiar with many events. For this, a wander through "downtown" was created that was designed to make the values and contents of the brand playfully tangible. In reference to the recommendation platform "TripAdvisor", the "RiedelAdvisor" offered the guests orientation. Familiar visualisations and descriptions ran through the whole world of experience and made visitors feel like going on a discovery tour.

MARC CAIN FASHION SHOW FALL/WINTER 2018
MARC CAIN GMBH, BODELSHAUSEN

Location
U3 Subway station and tunnel Potsdamer Platz, Berlin

Client
Marc Cain GmbH, Bodelshausen

Month / Year
January 2018

Duration
1 day

Direction / Coordination
Adelinde Knorr (Choreography), Marc Cain GmbH, Bodelshausen

Architecture / Design / Graphics / Decoration
Nowadays GmbH, Berlin; Marc Cain GmbH, Bodelshausen

Lighting
Nowadays GmbH, Berlin

Films
Streampark GmbH & Co. KG, Berlin

Music
Tom Peters

Artists / Show acts
Iconic Management GmbH & Co.KG, Berlin; Modelwerk Modelagentur GmbH, Hamburg; M4 Models Management GmbH, Hamburg; Mega Models Agency, Hamburg; Spin Model Management GmbH, Hamburg; Seeds Management GmbH, Berlin; Munich Models GmbH, Munich

Catering
Dahlmann Catering, Munich

Realisation
Studio Hamburg

Photos
Various (Owned by Marc Cain GmbH, Bodelshausen)

Um die Marc Cain Herbst/Winter-Kollektionen 2018 zu präsentieren, lud die Modemarke in das U3 Berlin. Die Location ist ein nicht genutzter U-Bahnhof direkt unter dem Potsdamer Platz. Der Tunnel mit seiner beeindruckenden Länge und besonderen Atmosphäre wurde zum Schauplatz einer Reminiszenz an die 80er-Jahre. Inspiriert vom legendären New Yorker „Studio 54" empfing Marc Cain seine Gäste unter dem Motto „Members Only".

IN EINEM UNGENUTZTEN BERLINER U-BAHNHOF ENTSTEHT EINE REMINISZENZ AN DIE 80ER-JAHRE.

A REMINISCENCE OF THE 80S IS CREATED IN AN UNUSED BERLIN UNDERGROUND STATION.

To present the Marc Cain autumn/winter collections 2018, the fashion brand issued invitations to U3 Berlin. The location is an unused underground station right under Potsdamer Platz. The tunnel with its impressive length and special atmosphere became the setting for a reminiscence of the 1980s. Inspired by the legendary "Studio 54" in New York, Marc Cain received their guests under the motto "Members Only".

Neon-Leuchtröhren und Schwarzlicht sowie 80er-Jahre-Beats schufen eine besondere Clubatmosphäre im Berliner Untergrund. Graffiti wurden innerhalb von eineinhalb Tagen kurz vor der Show von Urban-Nation-Künstlern vor Ort auf Leinwände aufgesprüht und prominent platziert. Knallige Farbakzente und glänzende Materialien in Kombination mit gedeckten Tönen und fluffigen Lockenmähnen ließen die 80er-Jahre auf dem Catwalk wiederaufleben.

Neon tube lights and black light, alongside 80s beats, created a special club atmosphere in the Berlin underground. Graffiti was sprayed on site onto canvases within one and a half days just before the show by Urban Nation artists and placed prominently. Loud colour accents and glossy materials, in combination with muted sounds and fluffy manes of curly hair brought the 80s back to life on the catwalk.

10 JAHRE TREI
MATT CIRCUS GMBH, COLOGNE

Location
TECHNIKUM, Mülheim an der Ruhr

Client
Trei Real Estate GmbH, Mülheim an
der Ruhr

Month / Year
September 2018

Duration
1 day

Dramaturgy / Direction / Coordination
MATT CIRCUS GmbH, Cologne

Architecture / Design
Tino Kubitza

Graphics
Art Direction Anna Müller, MATT CIRCUS
GmbH, Cologne

Lighting / Media
BIMAGOTEC OHG, Essen

Films
Marius Milinski, Passion Victim GmbH,
Cologne

Music
Jochen Peters

Artists / Show acts
Futurist Richard van Hooijdonk (Speaker)

Decoration
BALLONI GmbH, Cologne

Catering
Broich Premium Catering GmbH; espresso-
agogo

Others
Fabian Stürtz (Photos)

Photos
Fabian Stürtz; Anna Müller (MATT CIRCUS
GmbH)

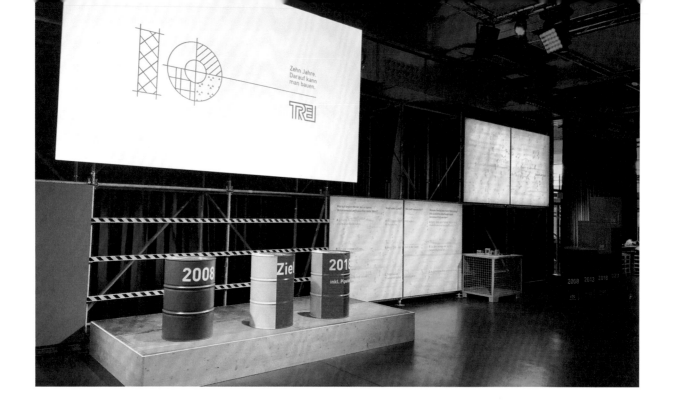

EIN JUBILÄUMSEVENT ALS INTERAKTIVE BAUSTELLE – UNKONVENTIONELL, KONSISTENT UND DETAILVERLIEBT UMGESETZT.

Anstatt klassischer Jubiläen mit Bühnenprogramm suchen Firmen heute nach anderen Formaten, die die Menschen aktiv für das eigene Themenfeld begeistern. Wie beispielsweise im Fall des 10. Jubiläums der Trei Real Estate. Die Immobiliengesellschaft der Unternehmensgruppe Tengelmann wollte 350 Gästen das abstrakte Produkt „Immobilien" auf unterhaltsame Weise näher bringen. Das Konzept von MATT CIRCUS spielte in diesem Sinne konsequent und konsistent mit Baustellen-Assoziationen. Vom Logo, das der Bauzeichenlehre entlehnt war, über typische Signalfarben, Flatterband und Baugerüste bis zur Hebebühne als Rednerpult.

Instead of traditional anniversary celebrations with a stage programme, companies today look for other formats that will stimulate interest in their particular topic area. An example of this is the case of the 10th anniversary of Trei Real Estate. The real estate business of the Tengelmann corporate group wanted to present the abstract product "real estate" to the 350 guests in an entertaining manner. In the interests of this, the concept of MATT CIRCUS played with building site associations consistently and systematically, from the logo that was derived from building symbols to typical signal colors, barrier tape and construction scaffolding and the lifting platform as a rostrum.

AN ANNIVERSARY EVENT AS AN INTERACTIVE BUILDING SITE – UNCONVENTIONAL, CONSISTENT AND REALISED WITH AN EYE FOR DETAIL.

Dabei durften die Gäste das Thema nicht nur visuell erleben, sondern an diversen Stationen interaktiv erkunden. So lernten sie Mitarbeiter anderer Standorte an einer Hörstation kennen. Eine Steckbrief-Installation mit Porträts von Mitarbeitern im Alter von 10 Jahren – ein humorvoller Bezug zum Jubiläum – gab spielerisch Aufschluss über ihre damaligen Berufswünsche und heutigen Positionen. Themeninseln verbanden aktuelle Projekte und Firmenschwerpunkte mit Getränken und Snacks. So wurden etwa Informationen über Handels- und Gewerbeimmobilien in ein Szenario mit Versatzstücken aus dem Supermarkt übertragen, Projekte wurden auf ausgestellten Produkten, wie einer Dosenpyramide, vorgestellt und gleichzeitig Getränke in den Regalen serviert. Die Themeninsel „Zukunft" fragte mit einer Installation nach den Meinungen der Gäste, die ihre Antworten an eine Wand nageln sollten. Ein unkonventionelles Konzept mit viel Liebe zum Detail, das den Gastgeber und seine Angebote sympathisch in Szene setzte.

The guests were able not only to experience the theme visually but also to explore it interactively at various stations. They therefore got to know employees from other branches at an audio station. An installation of profiles presenting employees in pictures at the age of 10 – a humorous allusion to the anniversary – gave information about what they wanted to become at the time and their current positions in a playful way. Theme islands combined current projects and firm focuses with drinks and snacks. For example, information about trade and commercial real estate was translated into a scenario based on elements from the supermarket, projects were introduced with exhibited products such as a pyramid of tin cans, while at the same time drinks were served. The theme island "Future" and its installation asked the opinions of guests who were to pin their answers to a wall. An unconventional concept with a love of detail that cast an amiable light on the host and what they have to offer.

A world first:
The Miele Dialog oven.

#revolutionaryexcellence

05:09

#newdimensions   #dialogoven

CREATING NEW DIMENSIONS – MIELE @ FUORISALONE 2018

FLORA&FAUNAVISIONS GMBH, BERLIN; WUNDERLAND DEUTSCHLAND GMBH, BERLIN

Location
Padiglione Visconti, Zona Tortona, Milano

Client
Miele & Cie. KG, Gütersloh

Month / Year
April 2018

Duration
several days

Project and Creative Lead
WUNDERLAND Deutschland GmbH, Berlin

Dramaturgy / Video and Kinetic Video Design / Video Production
flora&faunavisions GmbH, Berlin

Graphics
Das Kartell GmbH, Berlin

Music / Sound Designw
KLING KLANG KLONG, Berlin

Catering
Berlin Cuisine

Others
e.w.enture GmbH (Implementation and Set building); adhoc engineering GmbH (Technical and architectural planning); CT Creative Technology (Technical execution); Stage Kinetic (Prism technology); Reply td (Data-driven marketing); Delasocial (Social media activation)

Photos
Eduardo Perez

Der Miele Dialoggarer wurde erstmals auf der IFA 2017 vorgestellt – mithilfe eines Marketingevents, das mit einem dramaturgischen Moment überraschen sollte. 2018 präsentierte sich der Dialoggarer auf der EuroCucina in Mailand und sollte wieder überraschen. Diesmal mit einem begehbaren, mehrdimensionalen und sinnlichen Markenerlebnis, das für Begeisterung sorgen und zur Verbreitung in den sozialen Medien beitragen sollte. Zentraler Teil des einwöchigen Side-Events war eine begehbare kinetische 360-Grad-Multimedia-Installation.

EINE KINETISCHE 360-GRAD-MULTI-MEDIA-INSTALLATION SOLL DAS INTERESSE FÜR DAS PRODUKT STÄRKEN.

A KINETIC 360-DEGREE MULTIMEDIA INSTALLATION IS DESIGNED TO PROMOTE INTEREST IN THE PRODUCT.

The Miele Dialog cooker was first presented at the IFA 2017 – with the help of a marketing event that was designed to surprise with a dramatic moment. In 2018, the Dialog cooker was presented at EuroCucina in Milan and was set to surprise once again. This time with a walk-through, multidimensional and sensory brand experience that was to spark enthusiasm and contribute to distribution on social media. The central part of the one-week side event was a walk-through kinetic 360-degree multimedia installation.

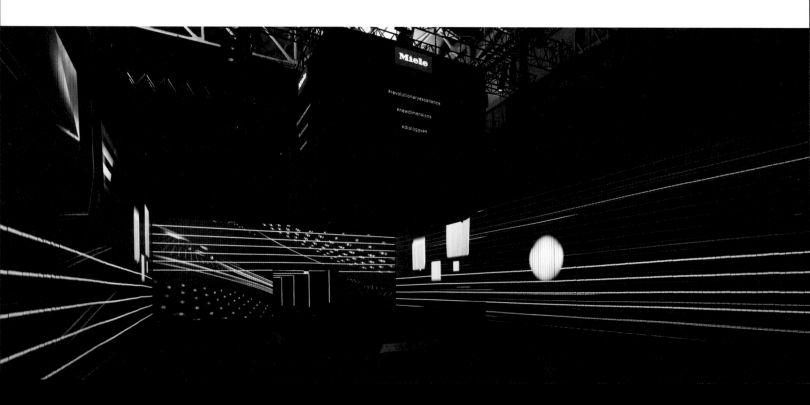

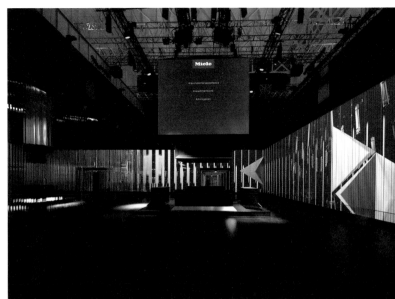

Auf einer Fläche von 1.000 Quadratmetern wurde eine kineti-sche Struktur aus 730 an den Wänden angebrachten Spiegel-prismen entwickelt. Sie dienten als Medienfläche, konnten aber auch die Wirkung eines Infinity Rooms samt überra-schenden Reflexionen und visuellen Effekten erzeugen. So entstand eine sich ständig ändernde Wand auf einer Länge von 80 Metern und einer Höhe von 5 Metern. Ein imposantes Erlebnis, das über Begeisterung das Interesse an der Marke und dem Produkt stärken und gleichzeitig die Besonderhei-ten dieser Innovation vermitteln sollte. Inhaltlich führten die multimedialen Sound- und Bildcollagen Schritt für Schritt durch die Produktkernthemen Excellence, Simplicity, Speedi-ness und Cooking Innovation. Nicht überraschend, dass die knapp 40.000 Besucher ihre dortigen Erlebnisse engagiert in den sozialen Medien teilten. Tagsüber war die Location samt Installation öffentlich zugänglich. Abends verwandelte sie sich in eine exklusive Dinner-Location für geladene Gäste.

In an area of 1000 square metres, a kinetic structure of 730 mirror prisms affixed to the walls was developed. They served as a media surface but could also generate the effect of an infinity room with surprising reflections and visual effects. This created a constantly changing wall 80 metres long and 5 metres high: an impressive expe-rience that was designed to reinforce interest in the brand and the product through enjoyment and at the same time convey the special features of this innovation. In terms of content, the multimedia sound and image collages led step by step through the key product themes of excellence, simplicity, speediness and cooking innovation. It was hardly surprising that the around 40,000 visitors shared their experiences there avidly on social media. During the day, the location and installation were open to the public. In the evenings, it transformed into an exclusive dinner location for invited guests.

DIGITAL2018
DO IT! GMBH, DUSSELDORF

Location
Koelnmesse, Hall 8, Cologne

Client
Telekom Deutschland GmbH, Bonn

Month / Year
November 2018

Duration
2 days

Dramaturgy / Direction / Coordination
DO IT! GmbH, Dusseldorf

Architecture / Design
Werft 6, Dusseldorf; Meiré und Meiré,
Cologne; DO IT! GmbH, Dusseldorf

Graphics
Matteng Grafik, Dusseldorf

Lighting
Neumann&Müller GmbH & Co. KG,
Esslingen am Neckar

Media
K16, Hamburg

Films
Pirates 'N Paradise GmbH, Dusseldorf;
Nordisch Filmproduction Anderson + Team
GmbH, Hamburg

Artists / Show acts
Black Eyed Peas; DJ Puentez

Decoration
DEKO-Service Lenzen GmbH, Lohmar

Catering
Kirberg Catering GmbH, Cologne

Realisation
DEKO-Service Lenzen GmbH, Lohmar;
Neumann&Müller GmbH & Co. KG,
Esslingen am Neckar

Photos
Markus Nass, Berlin; Fabian Stürtz,
Cologne; Lukas Palik Fotografie, Dusseldorf

EUROPAS FÜHRENDE DIGITALISIERUNGS-INITIATIVE BIETET INFORMATIONEN UND KONTAKTE AUF ENTSCHEIDER-LEVEL.

Eine Strategie, die man immer öfter sieht: Unternehmen und Marken veranstalten eigene Messen oder Konferenzen – und treten nicht selten mit großen Messeveranstaltern in Konkurrenz. Mit der DIGITAL2018 geht die Deutsche Telekom einen etwas anderen Weg: das Event ist eine Initiative der Telekom und wurde mit der Agentur DO IT! und diversen Partnern realisiert. Nach sechs regionalen Digital-X-Events als Tour durch Deutschland folgte das große Festival zum Thema Digitalisierung in der Koelnmesse. Es lockte 7.000 Besucher an und sollte DAX-Unternehmen, den deutschen Mittelstand, Start-ups, Lenker und Denker aus der Politik und junge Akademiker zusammenführen.

A strategy seen with increasing frequency: companies and brands hold their own trade fairs or conferences – often competing with major trade fair organisers. The Deutsche Telekom takes a somewhat different approach with the DIGITAL2018: the event is an initiative by Telekom and was realised with the agency DO IT! and various partners. Six regional Digital X events as a tour through Germany were followed by the major festival at Koelnmesse on the topic of digitalisation. It drew 7000 visitors and was to bring together DAX companies, German medium-sized enterprises, start-ups, drivers and thinkers from politics and young academics.

EUROPE'S FOREMOST DIGITALISATION INITIATIVE PROVIDES LEADERS WITH INFORMATION AND CONTACTS.

Verteilt auf zwei Tage bot die DIGITAL2018 eine Content-Plattform mit Vorträgen, Diskussionen, Panels und Keynotes wie zum Beispiel von Apple-Gründer Steve Wozniak. Viele verschiedene Partner präsentierten im interaktivem Ausstellungsbereich innovative Produkte und Services. Daneben gab es eine Schnittstelle für junge Akademiker, die Verleihung der Digital Champions Awards, einen Netzwerk-Lunch und ein Executive Netzwerkdinner für 2.000 Personen in den Themenrestaurants der Partnerunternehmen. Den Abschluss bildete ein Livekonzert der Black Eyed Peas. Eine eigene App unterstützte die Besucher bei der Erkundung und Planung vor Ort. Livestreams, ein Newsblog und Social-Media-Präsenz informierten Interessierte im Internet.

Spread over two days, DIGITAL2018 offered a content platform with presentations, discussions, panels and keynotes, such as by the Apple founder Steve Wozniak. Innovative products and services were presented by various partners in an interactive exhibition area. Alongside this, it included an interface for young academics, the presentation of the Digital Champions Awards, a network lunch and an executive network dinner for 2000 persons in the themed restaurants of the partner companies. The conclusion was formed by a live concert by the Black Eyed Peas. A designated app helped the visitors to explore and plan on site. Livestreams, a news blog and social media presence informed those interested on the Internet.

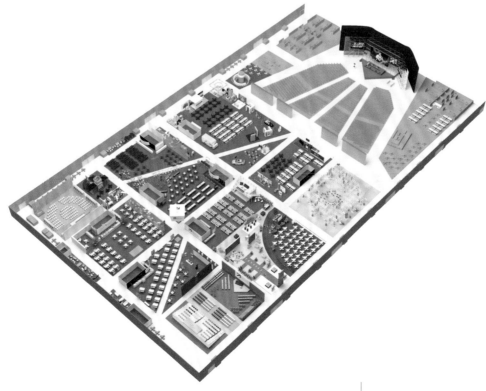

Jede Zielgruppe hat unterschiedliche Bedürfnisse und Erwartungen. Dementsprechend sind Eventkonzepte im Idealfall nicht nur auf den Absender, sondern vor allem auf die Empfänger zugeschnitten.

PRESS: SÄMTLICHE VERTRETER DER MEDIEN, ALSO NATIONALE UND INTERNATIONALE JOURNALISTEN (TV, PRINT, RADIO), BLOGGER, INFLUENCER – ALL JENE MULTIPLIKATOREN, DIE DAS SUJET BEHERRSCHEN UND INHALTE GEKONNT WEITERTRAGEN SOLLEN. DASS BEI DIESER ZIELGRUPPE LIVE-KOMMUNIKATION AN ERSTER STELLE STEHT, IST SELBSTVERSTÄNDLICH ...

Each target group has different requirements and expectations. Event concepts are therefore ideally not only geared towards the addressor, but especially towards the recipients.

PRESS: ALL REPRESENTATIVES OF THE MEDIA, NATIONAL AND INTERNATIONAL JOURNALISTS (TV, PRINT, RADIO), BLOGGERS, INFLUENCERS – ALL THE DISSEMINATORS WHO MASTER THE SUBJECT AND CAN SPREAD CONTENT EXPERTLY. IT GOES WITHOUT SAYING THAT LIVE COMMUNICATION IS KEY WITH THIS TARGET GROUP ...

BMW VISION iNEXT WORLD FLIGHT
VOK DAMS EVENTS GMBH, WUPPERTAL

Location
Airports MUC, JFK, SFO, PEK, Munich,
New York, San Francisco, Beijing

Client
BMW Group, Munich

Month / Year
September 2018

Duration
5 days

Dramaturgy / Direction / Coordination
VOK DAMS Events & Live-Marketing,
Munich

Architecture / Design
architects company, Munich

Lighting
macom NIYU, Berlin

Media
congaz Creative Media Production,
Dusseldorf

Photos
Enes Kucevic, Olching

Üblicherweise werden Pressevertreter für Produktpräsentationen aus aller Welt eingeflogen. Für das Konzeptfahrzeug BMW VISION iNEXT drehte VOK DAMS diesen Ansatz um: Anstatt an einer festen Location eine Produktpräsentation zu realisieren, brachten sie das neue BMW-Flaggschiff zu den Pressevertretern – in einem Flugzeug. Denn 2018 flog das neue BMW-Konzeptfahrzeug um die Welt.

ANSTATT DIE PRESSE EINZUFLIEGEN, WIRD EIN AUTO IN EINEM AUSSERGEWÖHNLICHEN SETUP UM DIE WELT GEFLOGEN.

INSTEAD OF FLYING THE PRESS IN, A CAR IS FLOWN AROUND THE WORLD IN AN UNUSUAL SETUP.

Media representatives are usually flown in from all around the world for product presentations. For the concept vehicle BMW VISION iNEXT, VOK DAMS turned this approach on its head: instead of realising one product presentation at a fixed location, they took BMW's new flagship car to media representatives – in an aeroplane. In 2018 the new BMW concept vehicle flew around the world.

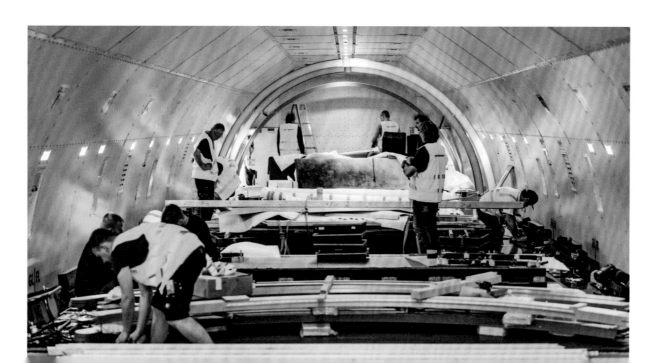

Für dieses Projekt wurde ein modernes Lufthansa-Fracht-
flugzeug, eine Boeing 777F, mit einem aufwendigen und
imposanten Präsentationsaufbau ausgestattet. Der Einsatz ein-
drucksvoller Licht- und Filminstallationen und einer Drehbüh-
ne sollte in seiner futuristischen Anmutung die Innovations-
kraft der Firma verdeutlichen. Inspiriert von Jules Vernes *In
80 Tagen um die Welt,* wurde der Wagen der Presse auf drei
Kontinenten, in vier Städten in nur fünf Tagen vorgestellt –
angefangen in der BMW-Heimatstadt München über New
York City und San Francisco bis Peking. Ein enger Zeitplan,
der es der Weltpresse erlaubte, das Auto fast gleichzeitig zu
erleben. Dieses unkonventionelle Event-Setup mit komplexen
Produktionsanforderungen und logistischen Herausforderungen erreichte aufgrund genau dieser Komplexität das an-
visierte Ziel: eine außergewöhnliche Medienberichterstattung
für die Marke und ihre Zukunftsvision.

For this project, a modern Lufthansa cargo plane, a Boeing
777F, was fitted with an elaborate and imposing presentation
structure. Impressive futuristic installations of film and light
and a turning table were designed to capture the essence
of the company's innovative power. Inspired by *Around the
World in 80 Days* by Jules Verne, the car could be presented
to the press on three continents, in four cities on only five
days – starting in BMW's home town Munich, via New York
City and San Francisco to Beijing. A tight schedule allowed
the world press to see the car almost simultaneously. This
unconventional event setup with complex product requirements and logistical challenges achieved its envisaged
objective precisely due to this complexity: exceptional media
reporting for the brand and its future vision.

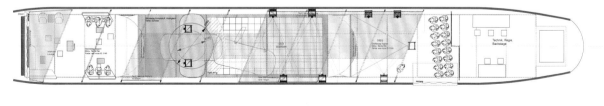

World Premiere
The New Mercedes-Benz
Stronger Than Time

WORLD PREMIERE OF THE NEW MERCEDES-BENZ G-CLASS
OLIVER SCHROTT KOMMUNIKATION GMBH, COLOGNE

Location
Michigan Theatre, Detroit

Client
Daimler AG, Stuttgart

Month / Year
January 2018

Duration
1 day

Concept / Direction / Dramaturgy / Architecture / Design / Graphics / Film Production
Oliver Schrott Kommunikation

Show Coordination
Mark Achterberg

Technical Direction
tec ViSiON GmbH, Frankfurt am Main

Lighting Design
rgb GmbH, Essen

Trade Fair Construction
Display International, Würselen

Lighting Supplier
PRG Production Resource Group AG, Detroit

Sound Supplier
Neumann&Müller GmbH & Co KG, Esslingen

Video & Broadcast Technology
AV-X GmbH, Oststeinbek

Special FX
Elements Entertainment GmbH, Bielefeld

Music
Inteativ production, Madrid

Photos
Daimler AG, Stuttgart; Andreas Keller

EIN IMPOSANTES BILD IN EINER SPEKTAKULÄREN LOCATION FÜR DIE ÄLTESTE MODELL-REIHE VON MERCEDES-BENZ.

Ein Marketingevent – ganz besonders eines für die Presse – sollte heute markante Bilder produzieren. Das hatte wohl auch Oliver Schrott Kommunikation im Sinn, als sie die Location für die Weltpremiere der neuen Mercedes-Benz G-Klasse im Rahmen der Detroit Auto Show 2018 auswählte: das ehemalige Michigan Theatre. Es wurde 1925 gebaut und ist mit seiner opulenten Kuppel ein wahrer Prachtbau. Damals bot es knapp 4.000 Zuschauern Platz und empfing Stars wie Frank Sinatra, Louis Armstrong und Doris Day. Doch seit Mitte der 70er-Jahre verfällt der Bau und fristet ein trauriges Dasein als Parkhaus.

A present-day marketing event – especially one for the press – should produce striking images. This is no doubt also what Oliver Schrott Kommunikation had in mind when choosing the location for the world premiere of the new Mercedes-Benz G-Class as part of the Detroit Auto Show 2018: the former Michigan Theatre. It was built in 1925 and is a truly magnificent building with its opulent dome. At the time, it seated around 4000 spectators and welcomed stars such as Frank Sinatra, Louis Armstrong and Doris Day. However, since the mid-1970s the building has been going to rack and carving out a miserable existence as a parking block.

AN IMPOSING IMAGE IN A SPECTACULAR LOCATION FOR THE OLDEST MODEL SERIES BY MERCEDES-BENZ.

Doch selbst nach 40 Jahren Verfall hat die Architektur nicht an Faszination verloren. Deswegen sah man die Location als idealen Ort für die G-Klasse – die am längsten produzierte Modellreihe von Mercedes-Benz – und ihren Produkt-Claim „stronger than time". Für die Präsentation wurde ein multimedialer Sturm der Elemente inszeniert. Herumwirbelndes Laub, Blitze und Donner, Wind und Feuer zeigten den Geländewagen in seinem natürlichen Umfeld. Ein Podest mit 40 Grad steilen Rampen ermöglichte die Live-Präsentation der Fahrdynamik und das zentrale Schlussbild: eine G-Klasse thront auf dem Gipfel, darüber die Renaissance-Kuppel des einstigen Theaters.

However, even after 40 years of decline, the architecture has not lost its fascination. For this reason, it was viewed as an ideal location for the G-Class – the Mercedes-Benz that has been produced for the longest – and its product claim "stronger than time". A multimedia storm of the elements was staged for the presentation. Swirling foliage, lightning and thunder, wind and fire showed the off-road vehicle in its natural environment. A platform with a ramp with an incline of 40 degrees enabled a live presentation of its driving dynamics and the central final scene: a G-Class crowns the peak with the Renaissance dome of the former theatre above it.

FUTURELAB@MERCEDES-BENZ TRUCKS
[MU:D] GMBH BÜRO FÜR EREIGNISSE, COLOGNE

Location
Branchen-Informations-Center (BIC),
Wörth am Rhein

Client
Daimler AG, Stuttgart

Month / Year
June 2018

Duration
1 day

**Dramaturgy / Direction / Coordination /
Architecture / Design / Music / Decoration**
[mu:d] GmbH, Cologne

Graphics
[mu:d] GmbH, Cologne + FVJ Content
Refinery GmbH, Berlin

Lighting / Media / AV Technology
dlp motive GmbH, Walzbachtal

Catering
Daimler Gastronomie GmbH, Wörth am
Rhein

Realisation
Sternbild03 GmbH, Dusseldorf

Photos
Kilian Bishop, Munich

Um Fach- und Wirtschaftsjournalisten einen exklusiven Blick hinter die Kulissen der Entwicklungsarbeit von Mercedes-Benz Trucks zu gewähren, lud das Unternehmen 2018 zum „FutureLab@Mercedes-Benz Trucks". Im Branchen-Informations-Center in Wörth am Rhein sollten Workshops und intensive Diskussionen über Visionen des Unternehmens informieren und auf kommende Weltpremieren im Rahmen der IAA einstimmen.

EIN INTENSIVES WORKSHOPFORMAT SOLL DIE PRESSE INFORMIEREN UND AUF KÜNFTIGE PRODUKTPREMIEREN EINSTIMMEN.

In order to grant specialist and economics journalists an exclusive glimpse behind the scenes of the development work of Mercedes-Benz trucks, in 2018 the company issued invitations to the "FutureLab@mercedes-Benz Trucks". At the sector information centre in Wörth am Rhein, workshops and intensive discussions were set up to provide information about the visions of the company and introduce the forthcoming world premieres as part of IAA.

Anstatt passiver Vorträge waren die knapp 100 Gäste eingeladen, proaktive Teilnehmer zu werden. Via Onlinetool konnten
sich die Journalisten vorab einen individuellen Tagesablauf
aus den angebotenen Themen-Workshops erstellen. In den
einzelnen Workshops mit Fachexperten der Daimler AG
wurde bewusst mit unterschiedlichsten didaktischen Metho-
den gearbeitet, um die Gäste möglichst intensiv einzubinden.
Im Sinne einer dynamischen, aktivierend-modernen Atmosphäre verzichtete die betreuende Agentur [m:ud] in der
2.250 Quadratmeter großen Halle auf Raumtrenner und schuf
eine ungezwungene Eventfläche. Durch die ergänzende
Nutzung der Silent-Conference-Technik sollte so eine offene
Arbeitswelt und der Charakter einer Zukunftswerkstatt umgesetzt werden. Der nur optisch abgetrennte Cateringbereich
bot über die Workshops hinaus Raum für individuelle Gesprä-
che und Networking.

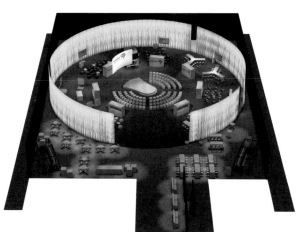

AN INTENSIVE WORKSHOP FORMAT IS DESIGNED TO INFORM THE MEDIA AND SET THE TONE FOR FUTURE PRODUCT PREMIERES.

Instead of passive presentations, around 100 guests were
invited to become proactive participants. Via an online tool,
the journalists could put together an individual daily schedule in advance from the theme workshops on offer. A wide
variety of didactic methods was used consciously in the
individual workshops with specialists from Daimler AG, in
order to involve the guests as intensively as possible. In the
interests of a dynamic, activating and modern atmosphere,
the appointed agency [m:ud] avoided room dividers in the
2250-square-metre hall and created a casual event space.
Through the complementary use of Silent Conference technology, the idea was to realise an open working world and
the character of a future workshop. The catering area only
separated off visually offered space for individual discussions and networking beyond the workshops.

JAGUAR F-PACE
"DARE TO CHALLENGE" SEASON 3
UNIPLAN GMBH & CO. KG, BEIJING

Location
Beijing Olympic Stadium

Client
*Jaguar Land Rover (China) Investment Co.
Ltd, Shanghai*

Month / Year
August 2018

Duration
1 day

Architecture / Design
Uniplan

AV & Lighting
*Echo-Blanc Culture & Communication Co.,
Ltd., Beijing*

Decoration
*Deyizhi (Beijing) Convention and Exhibition
Service Co., Ltd., Beijing*

Others
*InSPE Event GmbH, Wiesbaden (Driving
stunt)*

Photos
Uniplan GmbH & Co. KG, Beijing

EIN SPEKTAKULÄRER STUNT INSZENIERT DIE LEISTUNG ZWEIER JAGUARMODELLE UND ERREICHT MILLIONEN ONLINE-ZUSCHAUER.

Im Rahmen der chinesischen „Dare to Challenge"-Serie von Jaguar F-PACE sollte eine spektakuläre und aufsehenerregende Aktion umgesetzt werden. Ziel war es, die Leistung des F-PACE SUV zu demonstrieren. In diesem Sinne realisierte Uniplan in nur 45 Tagen von der Nominierung bis zum Veranstaltungstag einen gefährlichen und mit solchen Wagenmodellen noch nie umgesetzten Stunt.

Within the framework of the Chinese "Dare to Challenge" series by Jaguar F-PACE, a spectacular and sensational event was to be realised. The aim was to demonstrate the performance of the F-PACE SUV. With this in mind, Uniplan set up, in just 45 days from nomination to event day, a dangerous stunt never performed before with car models of this kind.

A SPECTACULAR STUNT HIGHLIGHTS THE PERFORMANCE OF TWO JAGUAR MODELS AND REACHES MILLIONS OF ONLINE VIEWERS.

Für diese Aktion wurde eine 8 Meter hohe und 150 Tonnen schwere Stahlkäfigstruktur gebaut. Die Wände der fast vertikalen Röhre hatten einen Winkel von 75 Grad. Gleich zwei SUVs, ein Jaguar F-PACE und E-PACE, sollten die enorm schrägen Wände der Röhre aus eigener Kraft befahren. Dabei mussten sich beide Autos im Abstand von nur 1,9 Sekunden in dem Stahlkäfig jagen. Beide Fahrer waren Kräften bis zu dreifacher Schwerkraft ausgesetzt. Ein wichtiger Aspekt war, dass die Leistung der Autos für diesen Stunt nicht künstlich verbessert wurde. Für den dramatischen Effekt wurden zwei telefonmastengroße Tesla-Spulen auf jede Seite des Käfigs positioniert. Während des Stunts sprühten sie donnernde Blitze. Die Aktion wurde live auf verschiedenen chinesischen Websites übertragen und erreichte über 15 Millionen Zuschauer.

For this event, a steel cage structure 8 metres high and 150 tons heavy was constructed. The walls of the almost vertical pipe had an angle of 75 degrees. Two SUVs, a Jaguar F-PACE and E-PACE, were to drive up the enormously steep walls of the pipe with their own power. The two cars had to chase each other in the steel cage with a gap of just 1.9 seconds. Both drivers were subjected to forces up to three times that of gravity. An important aspect was that the cars' performance was not artificially enhanced for this stunt. For dramatic effect, two Tesla spools the size of telephone masts were positioned on each side of the cave. During the stunt, thundering lightning was spraying. The event was transmitted live on various Chinese websites and has reached over 15 million viewers.

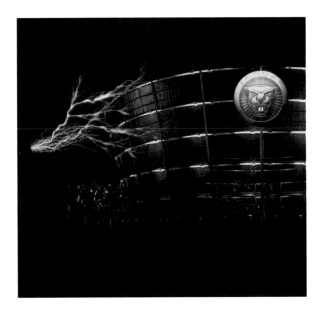

WORLD PREMIERE OF THE NEW MERCEDES-BENZ A-CLASS
OLIVER SCHROTT KOMMUNIKATION GMBH, COLOGNE

Location
Kromhouthal Amsterdam

Client
Daimler AG, Stuttgart

Month / Year
February 2018

Duration
1 day

Concept / Direction / Dramaturgy / Architecture / Design / Graphics / Film Production
Oliver Schrott Kommunikation

Show Coordination
Mark Achterberg

Technical Direction
tec ViSiON GmbH, Frankfurt am Main

Lighting Design
rgb GmbH, Essen

Trade Fair Construction / Graphic Production
Klartext GmbH, Willich

Lighting Technology
PRG Production Resource Group AG, Hamburg

Sound Technology
Neumann&Müller GmbH & Co.KG, Esslingen

Media Technology
AV-X GmbH, Oststeinbek

Decoration
Das Schauwerk GmbH, Freiberg am Neckar

Catering
De BorrelFabriek, Amsterdam

Photos
Daimler AG, Stuttgart; Andreas Keller

A PRESS EVENT WITHOUT A STRICT PROCEDURE BUT WITH A CASUAL ATMOSPHERE AND INDIVIDUAL CREATIVE POSSIBILITIES.

Zwanglos, locker und offen – so soll die Atmosphäre heutiger Marketingevents sein. Selbst im eher klassischen Bereich der Pressepräsentationen. Ein Beispiel dafür ist die Weltpremiere der neuen Mercedes-Benz A-Klasse in Amsterdam. Oliver Schrott Kommunikation entwickelte ein Konzept, das sich einem ungezwungenen Convention-Stil verschrieben hatte und den Gästen inhaltlich, räumlich und zeitlich Freiräume ließ. Tagsüber konnten die Gäste zwischen verschiedenen Programmpunkten frei wählen – zwischen Workshops und Vorträgen, Besichtigungen und Gesprächen oder dem Besuch eines angesagten Co-Working-Space. Inhaltlich ging es sowohl um die neue A-Klasse als auch um das neue Trendviertel Amsterdam Noord.

Casual, informal and open – this is what the atmosphere of present-day marketing events should be, even in the rather conventional area of press presentations. The world premiere of the new Mercedes-Benz A-Class in Amsterdam is an example of this. Oliver Schrott Kommunikation developed a concept that was built on a leisurely convention style and gave the guests freedom in terms of content, space and time. During the day, they could choose freely between various programme items – workshops and presentations, visits and discussions, or a visit to a trendy co-working space. The content was both about the new A-Class and the new trend district Amsterdam Noord.

EIN PRESSEEVENT OHNE STARREN ABLAUF, DAFÜR MIT LOCKERER ATMOSPHÄRE UND INDIVIDUELLEN GESTALTUNGS-MÖGLICHKEITEN.

The central feature of the afternoon programme was the "A Campus" in the Kromhouthal, a former shipbuilding hall. The car's highlights were presented there in a style reminiscent of a city district in a shop and café setting. At the "Multimedia Store", visitors found out everything about the new intuitive multimedia system MBUX capable of learning. In the "Lounge", guests experienced the interior of the A-Class at close quarters via virtual reality. And the "Garage" offered all information about the latest technology of the compact four-door model. The staging was of a casual and unconventional nature –consistent with its young target group and the atmosphere of the entire event.

Zentrum des Nachmittagsprogramms war der „A Campus" in der Kromhouthal, einer früheren Schiffbauhalle. Dort wurden die Highlights des Wagens im Stile eines Stadtviertels in inszenierten Geschäften und Cafés präsentiert. So erfuhren Besucher im „Multimedia Store" alles über das neue intuitive und lernfähige Multimedia-System MBUX. In der „Lounge" erlebten Gäste das Interieur der A-Klasse via Virtual Reality hautnah. Und die „Garage" bot alle Infos zur neuesten Technik des kompakten Viertürers. Die Inszenierung war ungezwungen und unkonventionell – passend zur jungen Zielgruppe und zum Flair der gesamten Veranstaltung.

INTERNATIONAL MEDIA LAUNCH
OF THE NEW BMW X2
HAGEN INVENT GMBH & CO. KG, DUSSELDORF

Location
Village Underground, Lisbon;
Hotel Palácio do Governador, Lisbon

Client
BMW Group, Munich

Month / Year
January – February 2018

Duration
2 weeks (7 groups, 2 days each)

**Dramaturgy / Direction / Coordination /
Architecture / Design / Graphics**
*HAGEN INVENT GmbH & Co. KG,
Dusseldorf*

Lighting / Media
Neumann&Müller, Taufkirchen

Decoration / Realisation
satis&fy AG, Karben

Photos
Mathias Hoffmann, Dusseldorf;
Tom Kirkpatrick, Starnberg

At the beginning of 2018, the new BMW X2 was presented to the media in Lisbon. The cheeky design of the car appeals to a target group young or young at heart, urban and active. Accordingly, the media event was supposed to be just as daring and surprising. The idea: a concept that plays and surprises with elements both traditional and modern, historical and urban, and generates a momentum of surprise.

CONSCIOUS JUXTAPOSITIONS OF TRADITION AND MODERNITY ARE DESIGNED TO PRESENT A DARING AND SURPRISING IMAGE.

The rebellious nature of the X2 was staged at the historical Hotel Palácio do Governador in a deliberately contradictory manner – with graffiti, a Playstation and Hololens experiences in historical rooms, characterized by portuguese wall tiles below traditional woodwork.

Anfang 2018 wurde der neue BMW X2 in Lissabon der Presse vorgestellt. Das freche Design des Wagens spricht eine junge und jung gebliebene, urbane und aktive Zielgruppe an. Mutig und überraschend sollte daher auch das Presseevent sein. Die Idee: ein Konzept, das mit traditionellen und modernen, historischen und urbanen Elementen spielt und überrascht.

In den Räumlichkeiten des altehrwürdigen Hotel Palácio do Governador wurde das rebellische Wesen des X2 bewusst widersprüchlich inszeniert – mit Graffiti, Playstation und Hololens-Erlebnis in historischen Räumen, geprägt von portugiesischen Wandkacheln unterhalb traditioneller Holzarbeiten.

BEWUSSTE BRÜCHE ZWISCHEN TRADITION UND MODERNE SOLLEN EIN MUTIGES UND ÜBERRASCHENDES IMAGE PRÄGEN.

Begleitet von Fado-Spielern gelangten die Gäste in historischen Trams zur Abendveranstaltung. Ziel war der von bunt besprühten Überseecontainern und aufgetürmten Bussen des Village Underground flankierte Platz unterhalb der berühmten Brücke Ponte 25 de Abril. Ein Stockbrotbacken am Lagerfeuer zwischen brennenden Ölfässern, musikalisch untermalt von den Klängen eines DJs, vollendete die kontrastreiche Einleitung in den Abend. Die Pressekonferenz und das Dinner fanden in einem temporären gläsernen Bau mit Kuppeldach statt – unter gefühlt freiem Himmel –, der die urbane Umgebung bewusst einschloss und mit Hunderten Vintage-Petroleumlampen und Kerzen eine behagliche Atmosphäre schuf. Kellner der alten Schule, mit schwarzem Frack, Weste und Fliege, servierten die typisch portugiesische Cataplana – und verkörperten so ideal das Motto: gewachsene Werte verbunden mit Mut zu Neuem.

Accompanied by fado players, the guests rode to the evening event in historical trams. Their destination was the place below the famous bridge Ponte 25 de Abril, which was surrounded by overseas containers covered in bright layers of graffiti and piled up buses of the Village Underground. A campfire between burning oil barrels where stick bread was baked to the sounds of a DJ completed a richly contrasting introduction to the evening. The press conference and dinner took place in a temporary glass building with a domed roof – much like being under an open sky –, which deliberately embraced its urban surroundings and created a comfy atmosphere with hundreds of vintage petroleum lamps and candles. Old school waiters, with a black tailcoat, waistcoat and bow tie, served the typical Portuguese Cataplana – and by doing so, embodied the motto in an ideal fashion: traditional values combined with a boldness of innovation.

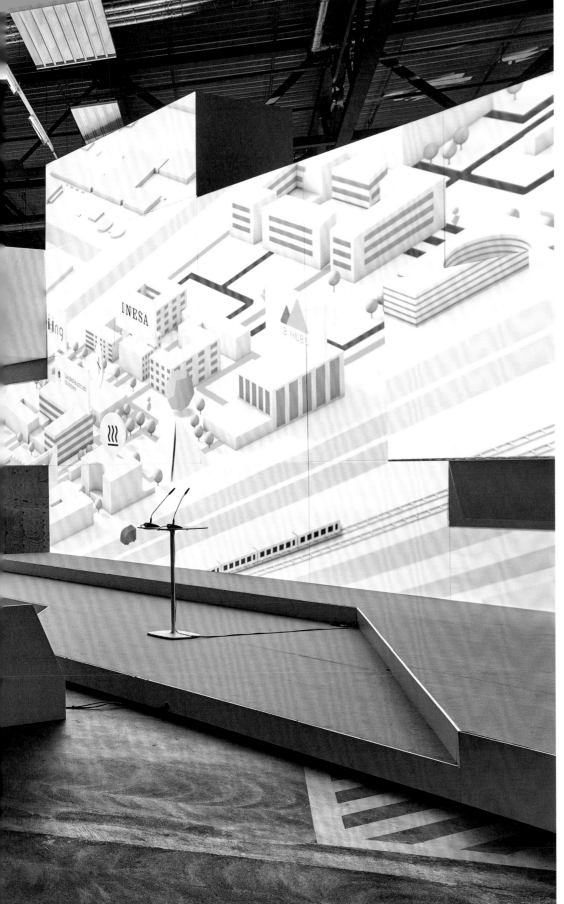

LABCAMPUS
TULP DESIGN GMBH, MUNICH;
WBLT VERANSTALTUNGSTECHNIK GMBH & CO. KG, OBERHAUSEN

Location
Freight hall, Munich Airport

Client
Flughafen München GmbH, Munich

Month / Year
March 2018

Duration
2 days

Dramaturgy / Direction / Coordination / Lighting / Media / Music / Catering
WBLT Veranstaltungstechnik GmbH & Co. KG, Oberhausen

Architecture / Design
TULP Design GmbH, Munich

Graphics
Pixelschickeria GmbH & Co. KG, Munich; TULP Design GmbH, Munich; Bloom GmbH, Munich

Films / Animation
Pixelschickeria GmbH & Co. KG, Munich

Realisation
Atelier Damböck Messebau GmbH, Finsing

Photos
Oliver Jung, Munich; Munich Airport

DAS KONZEPT UND DIE PLÄNE DES KÜNFTIGEN LABCAMPUS WERDEN FÜR EINEN TAG RÄUMLICH ERLEBBAR.

Am Münchner Flughafen wird in den nächsten Jahren ein unternehmens- und branchenübergreifendes Ideenzentrum entstehen: der LabCampus. Das Projekt soll Wissensträger, Global Player und Start-ups an einem internationalen Verkehrsknoten zusammenbringen. Beim offiziellen Launch-event sollten das Konzept kommuniziert und die geplanten Aspekte erlebbar gemacht werden. In einer Frachthalle des Flughafens setzte TULP gemeinsam mit WBLT Veranstaltungstechnik und der Pixelschickeria ein multimediales Raumkonzept um.

A cross-company and cross-sector ideas centre will be developed at Munich airport over the forthcoming years: the LabCampus. The project is designed to bring knowledge carriers, global players and start-ups together at an international transport hub. The concept was to be communicated and planned aspects to be introduced at an official launch event. In a freight hall of the airport, TULP together with WBLT Veranstaltungstechnik and Pixelschickeria implemented a multimedia spatial concept.

CONCEPT AND PLANS FOR THE FUTURE LABCAMPUS COME TO LIFE FOR A DAY IN A SPATIAL SETTING.

Überdimensionale kubische Strukturen bildeten das räumliche Hauptmerkmal. Sowohl die Bühne als auch der weitere Eventbereich wurden mithilfe von Mediatecture zum begehbaren dreidimensionalen Kino. Zahlreiche Projektionsflächen und architektonische Themeninseln machten den LabCampus-Gedanken erlebbar: schicke Bars, Workspaces, angedeutete Lofts und ein in Szene gesetzes Modell des LabCampus. Die inszenierte Fracht-halle diente dem Flughafen München auf facettenreiche Weise, potenzielle Kunden und spätere Nutzer auf die kommenden Möglichkeiten einzustimmen.

Oversized cubed structures formed the main spatial feature. Both the stage and the broader event area were turned into a three-dimensional walkable cinema by means of mediatecture. Numerous projection surfaces and architectural theme islands made the idea of the LabCam-pus come alive: fancy bars, workspaces, indicated lofts and a staged model of the LabCampus. For Munich Airport, this freight hall staging offered a variety of facets helping to familiarize potential customers and future users with the possibilities ahead.

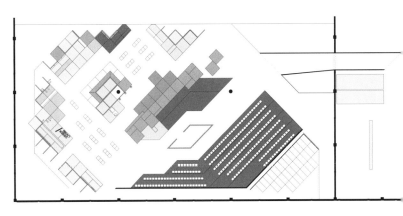

WORLD PREMIERE OF THE MERCEDES-BENZ VISION URBANETIC
OLIVER SCHROTT KOMMUNIKATION GMBH, COLOGNE

Location
Bella Center Copenhagen

Client
Daimler AG, Stuttgart

Month / Year
September 2018

Duration
1 day

Awards
Gold at BrandEx Award 2019

Concept / Direction / Dramaturgy / Architecture / Design / Graphic + Film Planning
Oliver Schrott Kommunikation

Show Coordination
Mark Achterberg

Technical Direction
Crossed Disciplines, Dortmund

Lighting Design
HELL Studio, Wuppertal

Trade Fair Construction
Klartext GmbH, Willich

Kinetics
Stage Kinetik GmbH, Castrop-Rauxel

Lighting + Sound + Media Technology
PRG Production Resource Group AG, Hamburg

Graphic Production
Stadelmayer Werbung GmbH, Kirchheim unter Teck

Film Production
Parasol Island GmbH; Dusseldorf; CFS Krug GmbH, Hamburg

Music
Jonathan Wulfes

Artists, Show-acts
Music At Event GbR

Decoration
Estilo Blomsterdesign ApS, Copenhagen

Catering
BC Hospitality Group A/S

Photos
Daimler AG, Stuttgart; Andreas Keller

Oliver Schrott Kommunikation entwickelte eine Idee, die den Gästen den Eindruck vermitteln sollte, durch Zeit und Raum zu reisen – auf einer 20 Meter breiten, drehbaren Tribüne, die Platz für 330 Gäste bot. In weniger als 10 Minuten drehte sich das Podest im Uhrzeigersinn und erzählte den Ablauf eines Vision-URBANETIC-Tages in der Zukunft. Der Van bewegte sich dabei auf einem stilisierten überdimensionalen Ziffernblatt von 12 bis 12 Uhr im Kreis. Die unterschiedlichen Funktionen des Konzeptfahrzeugs und die dahinterstehende Vision wurden so als umfassende Erfahrung inszeniert – und im Sinne einer umfangreichen medialen Berichterstattung um ein kinetisches Element bereichert.

Der Vision URBANETIC ist ein neues Mobilitätskonzept von Mercedes-Benz Vans. Der autonom fahrende Wagen ist für den Stadtverkehr der Zukunft entwickelt worden und kann sowohl für den Gütertransport als auch für die Personenbeförderung eingesetzt werden. Das Konzept des Vision URBANETIC sieht vor, dass er 24 Stunden lang 7 Tage die Woche unterwegs sein soll. Es basiert auf einem elektrisch betriebenen, fahrerlosen Chassis, das Aufbauten für unterschiedliche Einsatzzwecke tragen kann. Diese Idee und das dazugehörige Ökosystem sollten Journalisten und Influencern im Rahmen einer Veranstaltung in Kopenhagen vorgestellt werden.

EINE DREHBARE TRIBÜNE ALS INSZENIERTE ZEITREISE UND IMPULS FÜR DIE MEDIALE BERICHTERSTATTUNG.

The Vision URBANETIC is a new mobility concept by Mercedes-Benz Vans. The autonomous car has been developed for the city traffic of the future and can be used both as a transport vehicle and as a passenger car. The URBANETIC's concept envisages that it will be on the road 24 hours a day 7 days a week. It is based on an electric driverless chassis that can support additions for various usage scenarios. This idea and its associated ecosystem were to be presented to journalists and influencers in Copenhagen as part of an event.

A ROTATING STAND SETS THE SCENE FOR A JOURNEY THROUGH TIME AND STIMULATES MEDIA REPORTING.

Oliver Schrott Kommunikation developed an idea that was supposed to give visitors a feeling of travelling through space and time – on a 20-metre-wide rotating stand offering space for 330 guests. In less than 10 minutes, the platform turned clockwise and recounted the unfolding of a Vision URBANETIC day in the future. Over the course of this, the van moved in a circle on a stylised oversize clock face from 12 to 12. The different functions of the concept vehicle and the vision behind it thus were staged as a comprehensive experience – and enriched with a kinetic element in the interests of comprehensive media reporting.

Jede Zielgruppe hat unterschiedliche Bedürfnisse und Erwartungen. Dementsprechend sind Eventkonzepte im Idealfall nicht nur auf den Absender, sondern vor allem auf die Empfänger zugeschnitten.

EMPLOYEES: MITARBEITER EINES ODER MEHRERER UNTERNEHMEN, DIE ZUMEIST MOTIVIERT, ZUSAMMEN-GESCHWEISST ODER GRUND-SÄTZLICH BESSER GESTIMMT WERDEN SOLLEN. DIESE ZIELGRUPPE BEDARF EINES BESONDEREN FEINGEFÜHLS, UM DIE ZIELVORGABEN DES MANAGEMENTS MIT DER EMOTIONALEN WAHRNEHMUNG DER MITARBEITER ZU VEREIN-BAREN UND DIE BEABSICHTIGTE BOTSCHAFT ZU KOMMUNIZIEREN.

Each target group has different requirements and expectations. Event concepts are therefore ideally not only geared towards the addressor, but especially towards the recipients.

EMPLOYEES: EMPLOYEES FROM ONE OR MORE COMPANIES WHO ARE USUALLY TO BE MOTIVATED, BROUGHT TOGETHER OR GENERALLY HAVE THEIR SPIRITS RAISED. THIS TARGET GROUP REQUIRES A SPECIAL TOUCH IN ORDER TO ALIGN THE AIMS OF THE MANAGEMENT WITH THE EMOTIONAL PERCEPTION OF THE EMPLOYEES AND TO COMMUNICATE THE INTENDED MESSAGE.

WELCOME **CURIOCIT**

Tagesprogramm

MERCK

14:00 uhr	Einlass
14:00 - 20:00 uhr	Verschiedene Attraktionen auf dem Gelände, im M-Sphere und im Merck Innovation Center
15:00 uhr	Eröffnung des Merck Innovation Center mit Livestream in die ganze Merck Welt
20:30 - 21:00 uhr	Enthüllung des CurioCity Viertels Nordeuropa und Livestream aus Darmstadt
21:00 - 21:20 uhr	Finale - Große Abschlussshow auf dem Emanuel-Merck-Platz
22:00 uhr	Ende der Veranstaltung

Kleinkunstbühne

15:40 - 16:10 uhr	KurzFormChaos - Improvisations-Theater
16:15 - 16:25 uhr	Bauchtanz Act - Alexandra Martinek
16:45 - 17:10 uhr	Beatbox Performance und Workshop
17:10 - 17:20 uhr	Bauchtanz Act - Alexandra Martinek
17:20 - 17:40 uhr	Sängerinnen - Duo Jasmin Vetter & Katharina Göbel
17:45 - 18:15 uhr	KurzFormChaos - Improvisations-Theater
18:20 - 18:40 uhr	Mobiler Pianist - Marcel Kuipers
19:00 - 19:20 uhr	Ferdi Karatas & Band
19:25 - 19:55 uhr	KurzFormChaos - Improvisations-Theater
20:00 - 20:15 uhr	Beatbox Performance und Workshop

350 JAHRE MERCK –
GLOBAL EMPLOYEE EVENT
FISCHERAPPELT, LIVE MARKETING GMBH, COLOGNE

Location
Company facilities, Darmstadt

Client
Merck KGaA, Darmstadt

Month / Year
April 2018

Duration
1 day

Dramaturgy
fischerAppelt, live marketing, Hamburg

**Direction / Coordination / Media / Artists /
Show acts**
battleROYAl GmbH, Berlin

Architecture / Design
WHITE ELEMENTS GmbH, Berlin;
Crossworksprojects, Berlin

Graphics
fischerAppelt, Hamburg

Lighting
Chris Moylan

Films
fischerAppelt play GmbH, Hamburg;
battleROYAL GmbH, Berlin

Music
battleROYAL GmbH, Berlin; Stephan Zeh
(Composition Merck Hymn)

Decoration / Realisation
Artlife GmbH, München

Catering
Feinkost Käfer, Munich

Photos
Lichtbildatelier Eva Speith, Darmstadt;
Nick Putzmann, Leipzig

Das Thema Neugier hatte für das Unternehmen Merck und seine Mitarbeiter-Events schon immer eine besondere Bedeutung. Auch im Rahmen des 350-jährigen Jubiläums sollte das nicht anders sein. Unter dem Motto „Always curious – Imagine the next 350 years" sollten alle Aktivitäten im Zeichen der Neugier stehen. Für das Global Employee Event entwickelte fischerAppelt ein digitales sowie analoges Konzept, das speziell auf die Zielgruppe Mitarbeiter ausgerichtet sein sollte: die „CurioCity", die Stadt der Neugier. Schon 3 Monate vor dem Event hatten die weltweit arbeitenden Mitarbeiter die Möglichkeit, in der digitalen CurioCity zusammenzukommen. In dieser als Stadt konzipierten Internetplattform konnten „Bewohner" in Wohngemeinschaften einziehen, Aufgaben lösen und Neues entdecken.

EINE DIGITALE STADT SOWIE 12 WELTWEIT STATTFINDENDE EVENTS BRINGEN ALLE MITARBEITER ZUM JUBILÄUM ZUSAMMEN.

The topic of curiosity has always had a special meaning for the company Merck and its employee events. It was to be no different in the context of the 350-year anniversary either. Under the motto "Always curious – imagine the next 350 years", all activities were designed to be characterised by curiosity. For the Global Employee Event, fischerAppelt developed a digital and analogue concept that was tailored specially towards the target group of employees: the "CurioCity", the city of curiosity. Already 3 months before the event, the employees working worldwide had the opportunity to get together in the digital CurioCity. On the Internet platform conceived as a city, "inhabitants" could move into residential communities, solve tasks and discover something new.

A DIGITAL CITY AND 12 EVENTS TAKING PLACE WORLDWIDE BRING ALL THE EMPLOYEES TOGETHER FOR THE ANNIVERSARY.

Am 18. April 2018 fanden an 12 internationalen Standorten individuelle und lokal adaptierte, 30-minütige Shows statt. Via Livestream und CurioCity-Plattform wurden Beiträge, Bilder und Eindrücke geteilt. Eine speziell komponierte Merck-Hymne diente als virtueller Staffelstab zwischen den Standorten. Am Hauptsitz in Darmstadt fand das große Event mit 10.000 Gästen statt. Auf einer Fläche von 10.000 Quadratmetern wurden getreu dem Stadtkonzept fünf Distrikte erbaut. Unterschiedliche Aktivitäten, ein Bühnenprogramm mit musikalischen und informativen Auftritten sowie Darbietungen der Mitarbeiter bildeten die Inhalte. Das abschließende Highlight war eine interaktive Show, die mit einem 700 Quadratmeter großen Fassadenmapping aus Inhalten der CurioCity-Plattform auf dem neuen Merck Innovation Center endete.

On 18 April 2018, individual and locally adapted 30-minute shows took place in 12 international locations. Contributions, images and impressions were shared via livestream and the CurioCity platform. A specially composed Merck hymn served as a virtual relay baton between the locations. The major event with 10,000 guests took place at the head office in Darmstadt. Five districts true to the city concept were built on an area of 10,000 square metres. A variety of activities, a stage programme with musical and informative performances, as well as contributions by the employees, formed the content. The concluding highlight was an interactive show that ended with a façade mapping spanning 700 square metres on the new Merck Innovation Centre with content from the CurioCity platform.

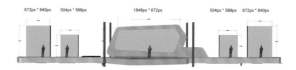

GROW THE NETWORK TOUR
[MU:D] GMBH BÜRO FÜR EREIGNISSE, COLOGNE

Location
Redblue Heilbronn

Client
Daimler AG, Stuttgart

Month / Year
April 2018

Duration
2 days

Dramaturgy / Direction / Coordination / Architecture / Design / Music
[mu:d] GmbH, Cologne

Graphics
[mu:d] GmbH, Cologne; Von Helden und Gestalten GmbH, Stuttgart

Lighting / Media
satis&fy AG

Decoration
Das Schauwerk GmbH & Co. KG, Freiberg

Awards
HR Excellence Awards 2018

Catering
Rauschenberger GmbH & Co. KG, Fellbach

Realisation
Klartext GmbH, Willich

Photos
Stephanie Trenz, Stuttgart

Mit der Initiative Leadership 2020 möchte die Daimler AG sich den neuen Entwicklungen und Herausforderungen innerhalb ihrer Führungs- und Unternehmenskultur stellen. Ein Teil dieser Initiative ist die Veranstaltungsreihe „Grow the Network Tour" (GTNT). Diese Veranstaltung soll den Kulturwandel initiieren, indem HR-Mitarbeiter relevante Anregungen erhalten, aber auch mit einem Change-Netzwerk aus Global Influencern bzw. Botschaftern verbunden werden. Die Agentur [m:ud] entwickelte mit diesem Ziel eine zweitägige Veranstaltung, die genügend Zeit und Raum für Austausch und ein gemeinsames aktives Lernen schaffen sollte.

AN EVENT IS DESIGNED TO STIMU-LATE AN INTERNAL CULTURE CHANGE THROUGH NETWORKING WITH GLOBAL INFLUENCERS.

EIN EVENT SOLL DEN INTERNEN KULTUR-WANDEL DURCH DIE VERNETZUNG MIT GLOBAL INFLUENCERN ANREGEN.

With the initiative Leadership 2020, Daimler AG would like to address the new developments and challenges within their management and corporate culture. Part of this initiative is the event series "Grow the Network Tour" (GTNT). This event is designed to initiate a culture change by providing HR employees with relevant suggestions, as well as being connected with a change network comprising global influencers and ambassadors. With this aim in mind, the agency [m:ud] developed a two-day event that was to create ample time and space for exchanges and shared active learning.

The first of a total of four worldwide stations took place in April 2018 in Heilbronn. The focus of the first day was on networking. The second day was to serve more in-depth individual content. The two groups were linked virtually as tandems in advance. At the beginning of the event, the tandem partners booked their individual programme from 15 workshops. The joint plenum was intended to encourage the tandems to spend time with a partner from the other group. Mutual support requirements therefore became apparent through the exchanges and networks could be strengthened. The spatial design was designed to promote a "community feeling" with open areas and the connecting plenum. The realisation as a Silent Conference and flexible catering with food trucks and "brown bag lunch" bags allowed the visitors to move around freely, to try out other workshops and to network extensively.

Die erste von insgesamt vier weltweiten Stationen fand im April 2018 in Heilbronn statt. Der Fokus des ersten Tages lag auf der Vernetzung. Der zweite Tag sollte der Vertiefung individueller Inhalte dienen. Im Vorfeld wurden die zwei Gruppen virtuell zu Tandems verknüpft. Zu Beginn der Veranstaltung buchten die Tandempartner ihr ganz individuelles Programm aus 15 Workshops. Das gemeinsame Plenum sollte die Tandems wiederum dazu animieren, Zeit mit einem Partner aus der jeweils anderen Gruppe zu verbringen. Gegenseitige Unterstützungsbedarfe konnten so im Austausch sichtbar und Netzwerke gestärkt werden. Die räumliche Gestaltung sollte mit offenen Flächen und dem verbindenden Plenum ein „Community Feeling" fördern. Die Umsetzung als Silent Conference sowie ein flexibles Catering mit Foodtrucks und „Brown Bag Lunch"-Tüten ermöglichten es den Besuchern, sich frei zu bewegen, in andere Workshops hineinzuschnuppern und ausgiebig zu networken.

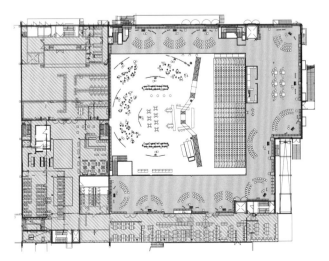

WELCOME TO Y/OUR NEXT LEVEL
ONLIVELINE GMBH – BÜRO FÜR KONZEPTION & INSZENIERUNG, COLOGNE

Location
Chia Laguna Resort, Domus de Maria

Client
Daiichi Sankyo Deutschland GmbH, Munich

Month / Year
May 2018

Duration
3,5 days

Awards
3rd Prize at Bea World Best Event Awards 2018

Dramaturgy / Direction / Coordination / Architecture / Design
onliveline GmbH, Cologne

Graphics
KonzeptZone Kommunikationsdesign, Cologne

Films / Media
MIM Fusion, Munich

Music
Audiomania, Frankfurt am Main

Artists / Show acts
Employees of Daiichi Sankyo

Catering
Hotel Chia Laguna, Domus de Maria

Realisation/ Decoration
DUGFEM, Röthenbach

Photos
onliveline GmbH, Cologne

Eine neue Unternehmenskultur darf nicht nur aus schönen Worten auf einmaligen Events bestehen. Sie muss in den Alltag implementiert werden. Für das Pharmaunternehmen Daiichi Sankyo sollte ein Mitarbeiterevent diese Verflechtung mit dem Alltag initiieren. Entsprechend der neuen, auf Co-Creation, Collaboration und Self-Empowerment basierenden Unternehmenskultur sollten die Mitarbeiter auf spielerische, explorative und emotionale Weise aktiviert werden. Unter dem Motto „Welcome to Y/OUR NEXT LEVEL" entwickelte onliveline in diesem Sinne ein Gamification-Event-Konzept, das bereits zwei Monate vor der Veranstaltung begann.

EIN GAMIFICATION-KONZEPT, DAS ZWEI MONATE ZUVOR BEGINNT UND EIGENVERANTWORT-LICHES HANDELN FÖRDERT.

Zentrales Ziel war die Anregung einer selbstverantwortlichen und interaktiven Informationsbeschaffung. Anstatt fertig aufbereiteter Veranstaltungsthemen arbeitete ein Netzwerk aus Mitarbeitern Themen eigenverantwortlich auf und brachte neue Inhalte ein. Eine Gaming-Plattform diente den Mitarbeitern als individuelle und inhaltliche Vorbereitung. Jeder Teilnehmer erstellte einen Avatar, schätzte persönliche Kompetenzen und Interessen ein und erstellte eine individuelle Sedcard für die Veranstaltung.

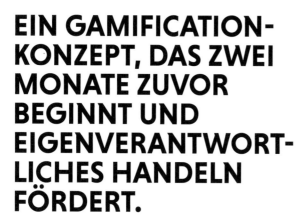

A new corporate culture cannot consist only of fancy words at one-off events. It must be implemented in everyday working life. For the pharmaceutical enterprise Daiichi Sankyo, an employee event was set up to initiate this integration into daily practice. In accordance with the new corporate culture based on co-creation, collaboration and self-empowerment, employees were to be activated in a playful, explorative and emotional manner. Under the motto "Welcome to Y/OUR NEXT LEVEL", onliveline developed a gamification event concept along these lines that already started two months before the event.

A GAMIFICATION CONCEPT THAT STARTS TWO MONTHS BEFOREHAND AND PROMOTES SELF-RELIANT ACTIONS.

The central objective was to stimulate the autonomous and interactive obtaining of information. Instead of ready-made event themes, a network of employees worked on topics themselves and brought in new content. A gaming platform served as individual and content preparation for the employees. Each participant put together an avatar, assessed personal competences and interests and compiled an individual Sedcard for the event.

Bei dem 3-tägigen Event wurde das Gaming-Konzept analog
fortgeführt – dramaturgisch unterteilt in die thematischen
Spannungsfelder „ME: Was habe ich davon?" und „WE:
gemeinsame Erfolgserlebnisse". Ein Online-Punktesystem
für die persönliche Weiterbildung, den Austausch von Wissen und selbstinitiierten Meetings sollte das Konzept und
Erleben unterstützen. Die Gaming-Plattform bündelte den
Punktestand, die bearbeiteten Themen und bot die Möglichkeit zum teamübergreifenden Austausch. Über 4.000
Kommentare untermalten das Ergebnis der Initiative.

The gaming concept was continued analogously at the
3-day event – dramaturgically divided into the thematic
fields of "ME: what's in it for me?" and "WE: shared success
experiences". An online points system for personal development, the exchange of knowledge and self-initiated
meetings were designed to support the concept and experience. The gaming platform pooled the points and themes
worked on and provided the opportunity for exchanges
between teams. Over 4000 commentaries accompanied
the result of the initiative.

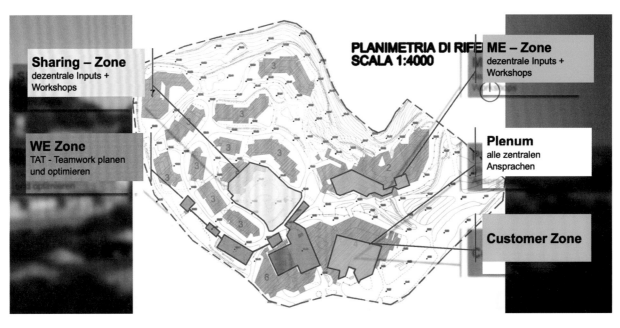

DIGITALLIFE DAY 2018
PULSMACHER GMBH, LUDWIGSBURG

Location
Werkzentrum West Ludwigsburg

Client
DigitalLife@Daimler, Daimler AG, Stuttgart

Month / Year
June 2018

Duration
1 day

Dramaturgy
pulsmacher GmbH, Ludwigsburg; Daimler AG, Stuttgart

Direction / Coordination / Architecture / Design / Graphics / Media
pulsmacher GmbH, Ludwigsburg

Lighting
Lautmacher Veranstaltungstechnik, Ludwigsburg

Catering
Schräglage GmbH, Stuttgart

Realisation
Bluepool GmbH, Leinfelden-Echterdingen

Photos
die Marquardt's, teamfoto MARQUARDT GmbH

EIN MITARBEITER-FESTIVAL SOLL INFORMIEREN, INSPIRIEREN UND DIE DIGITALE TRANS-FORMATION SICHTBAR MACHEN.

Der DigitalLife Day von Daimler hat gleich zwei Zielsetzungen. Er soll Mitarbeiter mit einem Tag voller Inspiration, Information und Innovation begeistern und zugleich die digitale Transformation im Konzern erlebbar machen. Jährlich werden 1.000 Mitarbeiter, die das Event besuchen dürfen, aus zahlreichen Bewerbungen per Zufall ausgewählt. 2018 lud Daimler mit einem Programm aus knapp 40 Rednern, 30 internen Marktständen, 10 Pitches, 5 Startups und 3 Partnerunternehmen in das Werkzentrum West Ludwigsburg. Das von pulsmacher entwickelte Eventkonzept inszenierte die Stadt als „Nervenzentrum der Digitalisierung". Eine Skylinewall schuf das Key Visual. Marktstände aus Gitterboxen und Europaletten sollten an kleine Häuserblöcke erinnern. Die Hauptbühne bildete den Marktplatz. Ein Weg zu den Nebenbühnen bzw. der Vorstadt wurde als Park umgesetzt.

The DigitalLife Day by Daimler has two objectives. It is designed to appeal to employees with a day full of inspiration, information and innovation and at the same time to enable to experience digital transformation within the corporation. Every year, 1000 employees are selected randomly from numerous applications to attend the event. In 2018, Daimler issued invitations to the Werkzentrum West Ludwigsburg with a programme comprising around 40 speakers, 30 internal market stands, 10 pitches, 5 startups and 3 partner companies. The event concept developed by pulsmacher staged the town as the "nerve centre of digitisation". A skyline wall provided the key visual. Market stands made of mesh crates and europallets were intended to evoke small housing blocks. The market square formed the main stage. A path to the side stages and the suburbs was realised as a park.

AN EMPLOYEE FESTIVAL IS DESIGNED TO INFORM AND INSPIRE AND TO MAKE THE DIGITAL TRANSFORMATION VISIBLE.

Inhaltlich bot der Tag neben Vorträgen von unter anderem Dr. Dieter Zetsche, Michel van der Bel (Microsoft), Edzard Overbeek (HERE) und Clare Jones (What3Words) Innovations-Pitches unter der Moderation von Amiaz Habtu. Zehn Teams hatten die Chance, im klassischen „Shark Tank"-Format eine Finanzierung für ihre Idee zu gewinnen. Mit einer App konnten die Teilnehmer ihre individuelle Agenda zusammenstellen. 2018 wurde erstmalig das Themenfeld „Art meets DigitalLife Day" in das Event integriert – mit der künstlerischen Ausgestaltung durch den Stuttgarter Künstler Robin Treier und einer A(rt)-Class, die live auf dem Event mit Künstler und Gästen entstand. Neu war ebenfalls ein nachhaltiger Ansatz: Nahezu alle eingesetzten Ressourcen und Materialien waren recycle- oder biologisch abbaubar. Der Foodcourt bot ausschließlich lokale und biologisch produzierte Speisen auf Palmblättern.

In terms of content, alongside presentations, the day offered innovation pitches moderated by Amiaz Habtu, including by Dr. Dieter Zetsche, Michel van der Bel (Microsoft), Edzard Overbeek (HERE) and Clare Jones (What3Words). Ten teams had the opportunity to win funding for their idea in the traditional "shark tank" format. An app helped participants to compile their individual agenda. In 2018, the theme of "Art meets DigitalLife Day" was integrated into the event for the first time – with an artistic arrangement by the Stuttgart artist Robin Treier and an A(rt)-class that came together live at the event with the artist and guests. Another new feature was a sustainability approach: Almost all the resources and materials used were recyclable or biodegradable. The food court offered exclusively local and organically produced foods on palm leaves.

SKAN 50 | BACKYARD PARTY
EVENT NOW GMBH, FREIBURG IM BREISGAU

Location
Messe Basel, Hall 3

Client
SKAN AG, Allschwil

Month / Year
September 2018

Duration
1 day

**Dramaturgy / Direction / Coordination /
Graphics / Media / Realisation**
EVENT NOW GmbH, Freiburg im Breisgau

Architecture / Design
EVENT NOW GmbH, Freiburg im Breisgau;
Karoline Hahn, Freiburg im Breisgau

Films
Fuchsrot Creative Media Production,
Freiburg im Breisgau

Lighting
DLP Motive, Walzbachtal

Music
VKKO, Munich; Schlagzeugmafia,
Mannheim; Franck Derouin, Paris

Artists / Show acts
Duo Flip 'n' Fly, Rotterdam; Marie
Bitarozcky, Berlin; Marc Gassert, Munich

Decoration
Machart Eventdesign GmbH & Co. KG,
Mühlheim bei Frankfurt am Main

Catering
Wassermann & Company AG, Basel

Photos
Felix Groteloh, Freiburg im Breisgau

EINE „BACKYARD PARTY" STATT KLASSISCHEM JUBILÄUMSEVENT BRINGT 600 INTERNATIONALE MITARBEITER ZUSAMMEN.

Klassische Jubiläumsformate, die frontale Bühnenshows, lange Reden und stundenlange Sitzzeiten beinhalten, sterben langsam aus. Selbst Gastgeber aus mittelständischen und vielleicht etwas traditionelleren Industriezweigen möchten ihren Gästen mehr Freiraum gönnen. So verzichtete auch das internationale Unternehmen SKAN AG aus der Reinraumtechnologiebranche auf ein klassisches Event, um sein 50. Firmenjubiläum zu feiern. Anstatt dessen sollte eine familiäre Veranstaltung ohne festes Programm und Ablaufzeiten entstehen.

Traditional anniversary formats that comprise frontal stage shows, long speeches and sitting for hours are slowly dying out. Even hosts from medium-sized and perhaps rather more traditional industrial sectors would like to give their guests more freedom for movement. The international company SKAN AG from the cleanroom technology sector also decided against a conventional event to celebrate its 50th company anniversary. Instead of this, there was to be an informal event without a fixed programme and schedule.

A "BACKYARD PARTY" INSTEAD OF A CONVENTIONAL ANNIVERSARY EVENT BRINGS 600 INTERNATIONAL EMPLOYEES TOGETHER.

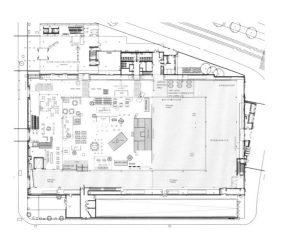

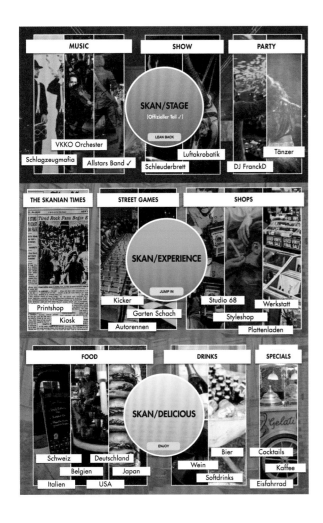

Das von EVENT NOW entwickelte Konzept der „Backyard Party" kombinierte das Flair eines New Yorker Hinterhofs mit der Schrillheit der 60er-Jahre. Durch die Platzierung von Foodtrucks, Seecontainern, Bäumen, Hecken, Liegewiesen, Laternen, Zebrastreifen und Litfaßsäulen entstanden Hinterhöfe, Straßen und Plätze. Palettenbars, Parkbänke, Oldtimer und Fahrräder kreierten kleine Spots zum Erkunden und Verweilen. Unterteilt in „SKAN STAGE", „SKAN EXPERIENCE" und „SKAN DELICIOUS", wurden inhaltlich Entertainment und Musik, Shops und Street Games sowie Speisen und Getränke aus sechs Nationen geboten. Auf ein zeitlich fest getaktetes Programm klassischer Natur wurde weitgehend und bewusst verzichtet. Der Fokus lag auf dem Austausch und Miteinander der 600 internationalen Mitarbeiter.

The concept of the "backyard party" developed by EVENT NOW combined the flair of a New York back yard with the shrillness of the 1960s. Placing food trucks, sea containers, trees, hedges, lawns, lanterns, zebra crossings and advertising columns created back yards, streets and squares. Pallet bars, park benches, vintage cars and bicycles created little spots for exploring and lingering. Divided into "SKAN STAGE", "SKAN EXPERIENCE" and "SKAN DELICIOUS", content was offered comprising entertainment and music, shops and street games, as well as food and drink from six nations. A firmly scheduled programme of a traditional nature was largely and consciously avoided. The focus was on exchanges and the gathering of the 600 international employees.

MERCEDES-BENZ GLOBAL TRAINING EXPERIENCE IBIZA 2018
STAGG & FRIENDS GMBH, DUSSELDORF; JANGLED NERVES GMBH, STUTTGART

Location
FECOEV Ibiza

Client
Daimler AG /Mercedes-Benz Global
Training, Stuttgart

Month / Year
February – April 2018

Duration
3 days per group

Awards
Galaxy Award 2018, Bea World Best Event
Awards 2018, Gold at International
Advertising Competition Golden Award
of Montreux 2019

Dramaturgy / Direction / Coordination
STAGG & FRIENDS GmbH, Dusseldorf

Architecture / Design / Films / Media
jangled nerves GmbH, Stuttgart

Graphics
storygraphers, Cologne

Lighting
PRG Production Resource Group AG,
Hamburg

Decoration
Artlife GmbH, Hofheim

Photos
Ernest O. Forstmark, Ibiza City

EINE OFFENE CONVENTION INFORMIERT ÜBER NEUE PRODUKTE UND DEN UMGANG MIT SOCIAL MEDIA.

The Global Training Experience (GTE) by Mercedes-Benz was held in Ibiza in 2018. 14,700 participants from all around the world were flown in for a day over a period of 11 weeks. The content focus was the market introduction of the new Mercedes-Benz A-Class with its new digital voice control, the so-called MBUX. Information and content were not only to be communicated in line with the buyer target group. The concept should also contain as many digital elements as possible in order to drive forward digital transformation within the corporation.

Die Global Training Experience (GTE) von Mercedes-Benz fand 2018 auf Ibiza statt. 14.700 Teilnehmer aus aller Welt wurden über 11 Wochen hinweg für einen Tag eingeflogen. Inhaltlicher Fokus war die Markteinführung der neuen Mercedes-Benz A-Klasse mit ihrer neuen, digitalen Sprachsteuerung, dem sogenannten MBUX. Informationen und Inhalte sollten dabei nicht nur entsprechend der Käuferzielgruppe kommuniziert werden. Das Konzept sollte auch möglichst viele digitale Elemente enthalten, um die digitale Transformation im Konzern voranzutreiben.

AN OPEN CONVEN-TION PROVIDES INFORMATION ABOUT NEW PRODUCTS AND INVOLVEMENT WITH SOCIAL MEDIA.

STAGG & FRIENDS entwickelte eine Austauschplattform im Stil einer Convention. Was der Mercedes-Benz IAA-Auftritt und die me.Convention für Kunden ist, wurde unter dem Namen Hey Mercedes für den Vertrieb realisiert. Ein Open-Space-Trainingscampus, das A_lements, sollte mit einer offenen Club-atmosphäre begeistern. Die Teilnehmer informierten sich über ihre eigenen Smartphones, auf inter-aktiven Spielflächen und mit unterschiedlichen Augmented-Reality-Formaten. Das Teilen und Kommentieren in den noch ungewohnten sozialen Medien sollte näher gebracht und gefördert werden.

STAGG & FRIENDS developed an exchange platform in the style of a convention. What the Mercedes-Benz IAA presen-tation and the me.Convention is for customers was realised under the name Hey Mercedes for sales. An open-space training campus, A_lements, was designed to inspire with an open club atmosphere. The participants informed them-selves with their own smartphones, on interactive gaming interfaces with various augmented reality formats. Sharing and commenting on the still unaccustomed social media were to be introduced and promoted.

Jede Zielgruppe hat unterschiedliche Bedürfnisse und Erwartungen. Dementsprechend sind Eventkonzepte im Idealfall nicht nur auf den Absender, sondern vor allem auf die Empfänger zugeschnitten.

EXPERTS: FACHPUBLIKUM, BRANCHENKENNER UND EXPERTEN, DIE AN EINEM GEMEINSAMEN THEMA INTERESSIERT SIND. DER AUSTAUSCH AUF FACHEBENE STEHT DABEI IM MITTELPUNKT UND PRÄGT DIE KOMMUNIKATION WESENTLICH. DIESE ZIELGRUPPE IST VORNEHMLICH AN DER VERMITTLUNG VON WISSEN INTERESSIERT, DIE WEIT ÜBER DIE WEITERGABE REINER INFORMATIONEN HINAUSGEHT.

Each target group has different requirements and expectations. Event concepts are therefore ideally not only geared towards the addressor, but especially towards the recipients.

EXPERTS: THESE ARE A SPECIALIST PUBLIC AND EXPERTS IN THE SECTOR WHO ARE INTERESTED IN A COMMON SUBJECT. THE FOCUS IS ON AN EXCHANGE AT EXPERT LEVEL, WHICH SHAPES THE COMMUNICATION SIGNIFICANTLY. THIS TARGET GROUP IS PRIMARILY INTERESTED IN THE TRANSMISSION OF KNOWLEDGE THAT GOES WAY BEYOND THE PASSING ON OF MERE INFORMATION.

GRAND OPENING OF THE QATAR NATIONAL LIBRARY
FISCHERAPPELT, QATAR

Location
Qatar National Library, Education City, Al Luqta St, Ar-Rayyan, Doha

Client
Qatar National Library / Qatar Foundation

Month / Year
April 2018

Duration
1 day

Awards
2 × Bronze at Bea World Best Event Awards 2018; Bronze at BrandEx Award 2019

Dramaturgy / Direction / Coordination / Media / Architecture / Design / Graphics / Films / Decoration / Realisation
fischerAppelt, Qatar

Lighting
Peter Heybutzki, ES:ME, fischerAppelt, Qatar

Music
fischerAppelt, Qatar; Dana AlFardan (Sounds of the Library); Qatar Philharmonic Orchestra

Arists
Inauguration Show: fischerAppelt, Qatar (Concept); Lichtfaktor, Cologne (Realisation); Hans-Christoph Mücke (Direction)

Catering
Four Seasons, Doha

Others
Andreas Cabral; Sascha Hinz (Technical planning)

Photos
Alex Klim Filmmaker; Doha, Qatar

MODERNE UND TRADITION INSZENIERT ZWISCHEN ANALOGEN BÜCHERN UND DIGITALER KOMMUNIKATION.

On 16 April 2018, Doha celebrated the Qatar National Library (QNL), the first national library to open in the 21st century. A place that not only houses texts thousands of years old but is also equipped with the latest technologies. An institution that is intended not only to serve as a curator for the spiritual heritage of the region but also as a communal space for the people of Qatar. This was to be communicated in a major opening show as well as an accompanying marketing campaign.

Am 16. April 2018 feierte Doha die Qatar National Library (QNL), die erste Nationalbibliothek, die im 21. Jahrhundert eröffnet wurde. Ein Ort, der nicht nur jahrtausendealte Texte beherbergt, sondern auch mit modernsten Technologien ausgestattet ist. Eine Institution, die nicht nur als Kurator für das geistige Erbe der Region, sondern auch als Gemeinschaftsraum für die Menschen in Katar dienen soll. Dies galt es in einer großen Eröffnungsshow sowie einer begleitenden Marketingkampagne zu kommunizieren.

MODERNITY AND TRADITION ARE STAGED BETWEEN ANALOGUE BOOKS AND DIGITAL COMMUNICATION.

FischerAppelt entwickelte dafür die Leitidee „Licht ist Wissen",
die mit verschiedensten Elementen zum Leben erweckt werden sollte. Von einem 70 Meter langen LED-Teppich mit einer
Reise durch Katar über CGI-Animationsvideos für die Social-
Media-Kommunikation bis hin zum Highlight, einer Eröffnungsshow mit Lichtartisten und eigener Musikkomposition.
Ein wichtiger Aspekt der Eröffnungsveranstaltung war es,
die Architektur des Gebäudes zu respektieren. So wurde die
Bühne in der Mitte der Bibliothek positioniert und die Seiten
als „digitale Bücherregale" inszeniert. Die Musiker des Qatar
Philharmonic Orchestra, die den Abend live untermalten,
wurden auf verschiedenen Ebenen zwischen den Regalen
platziert. Ein 60-minütiges Bühnenprogramm kombinierte drei
Filme mit kurzen Reden. Tradition und Moderne sollten so
in ausgewogener Balance miteinander verbunden werden.

FischerAppelt developed the guiding idea of "Light is knowledge" for this purpose, which was to be brought to life
with a wide variety of elements. From a 70-metre-long LED
carpet with a journey through Qatar and CGI animation
videos for social media communication through to the
highlight, an opening show with light artists and music composed especially. An important aspect of the opening event
was to respect the architecture of the building. The stage
was therefore positioned in the middle of the library and the
sides were staged as "digital bookshelves". The musicians
from the Qatar Philharmonic Orchestra who accompanied
the evening live were positioned on different levels between the shelves. A 60-minute stage programme combined
three films with short speeches. Tradition and modernity
were thus to be combined in a harmonious balance.

BEST CARS 2018
VISUELL STUDIO FÜR KOMMUNIKATION GMBH, STUTTGART

Location
ICS Internationales Congresscenter Stuttgart

Client
Motor Presse Stuttgart GmbH & Co. KG, Stuttgart

Month / Year
January 2018

Duration
1 day

Dramaturgy / Direction / Coordination / Architecture / Design / Graphics / Media / Decoration
VISUELL Studio für Kommunikation GmbH, Stuttgart

Lighting
Neumann&Müller, Esslingen (Light and Sound technology); PASS AV, Kornwestheim (Projection technique)

Catering
Aramark, Stuttgart

Photos
VISUELL Studio für Kommunikation GmbH (Johannes Eitelbuß)

Jedes Jahr wählen die Leser des Magazins *AUTO MOTOR UND SPORT* die besten Autos des Jahres und beantworten Fragen rund um das Thema Mobilität. Die Ergebnisse und Siegerautos werden im Rahmen einer Galaveranstaltung präsentiert. Eingeladen sind Führungskräfte und Marketingverantwortliche nationaler und internationaler Automarken. Ergänzend dazu wollte der Verlag 2018 seine neue Unternehmensstrategie kommunizieren und somit auch die Preisverleihung in neuem Licht erstrahlen lassen. VISUELL übernahm die Umsetzung – von Einladungskarten über Raumgestaltung und Trophäendesign bis zur technischen Planung und Eventregie – und setzte dabei ein ganzheitliches Konzept mit klarer Linie um.

Every year, readers of the magazine *AUTO MOTOR UND SPORT* vote for the best cars of the year and answer questions surrounding the topic of mobility. The results and winning cars are presented as part of a gala event. Managers and those responsible for marketing at national and international car brands are invited. In addition, in 2018 the publishing house wanted to communicate its new corporate strategy and thereby also cast a new light on the prize awards. VISUELL was appointed for the realisation – from invitation cards to spatial design and trophy design, technical planning and event management – implementing an overall concept with a clear direction.

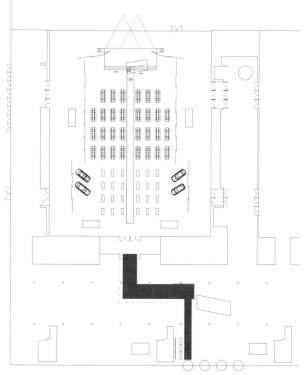

60 BEWEGLICHE CUBE-LEUCHTEN INSZENIEREN DEN RAUM UND SCHAFFEN UNTERSCHIEDLICHE ATMOSPHÄREN.

60 MOVABLE CUBE LIGHTS STAGE THE SPACE AND CREATE DIFFERENT ATMOSPHERES.

The topic of light formed the common thread. The spatial highlight were 60 cubed lights floating in the event space. They could be controlled individually during the show and incorporated into the staging. At the beginning, the lights were raised several metres into the air and opened up a view of the stage. For the subsequent dinner, the lights were lowered to just above the tables and immersed the space in a cosy atmosphere. The stage show played on the theme of light with light contours like cut-outs. It was not until the moment the winners were announced that they rounded out and illuminated the prize winner. Individually composed soundtracks for each of the 11 vehicle categories accompanied the event as an audio element. A highlight of the stage programme was a specially programmed gesture control for the presentation by the chief editorship.

Das Thema Licht bildete den roten Faden. Räumliches High-light waren 60 im Raum schwebende kubische Leuchten. Sie konnten während der Show einzeln angesteuert und in die Inszenierung einbezogen werden. Zu Beginn fuhren die Lampen um mehrere Meter nach oben und gaben den Blick auf die Bühne frei. Zum anschließenden Essen fuhren die Lichter bis knapp über die Tische herunter und tauchten den Raum in eine gemütliche Atmosphäre. Die Bühnenshow bespielte das Thema Licht mit ausschnitthaften Leuchtkonturen. Erst im Moment der Gewinnerbekanntgabe vervollständigten sie sich und gaben den Preisträger zu erkennen. Individuell komponierte Klänge für die jeweils 11 Fahrzeugkategorien untermalten das Event auditiv. Ein Höhepunkt des Bühnen-programms war eine eigens programmierte Gestensteuerung für den Vortrag der Chefredaktion.

MAGENTA URBAN GARDEN@TOA 2018
PHOCUS BRAND CONTACT
GMBH & CO. KG, NUREMBERG

Location
Altes Funkhaus, Berlin

Client
T-Systems International GmbH, Bonn

Month / Year
June 2018

Duration
several days

Dramaturgy / Direction / Coordination / Architecture / Design / Graphics
PHOCUS BRAND CONTACT GmbH & Co. KG, Nuremberg: Anja Osswald (Dramaturgy), Kati Kindrat (Direction, Coordination), Eva Köhler (Architecture, Design, Graphics)

Artists / Show acts
TAPEOVER Tape Artists, Berlin; URBAN LAB, Nuremberg

Decoration / Realisation
DEKO-Service Lenzen GmbH, Lohmar

Catering
Lebenswelten Restaurations GmbH, Berlin

Photos
Pascal Rohé (Film & Photography)

ZIELGRUPPEN-ORIENTIERTE HANDS-ON-ERLEBNISSE SOLLEN INTER-AKTIONEN SCHAFFEN UND DAS IMAGE STÄRKEN.

Das Tech Open Air Festival (TOA) ist Europas größtes inter-disziplinäres Technologiefestival. Das in Berlin stattfindende und angesagte Event zieht jährlich bis zu 15.000 Besucher an – der ideale Ort, um als Technologiefirma mit seiner enga-gierten Zielgruppe in Kontakt zu kommen. So wollte sich dort auch T-Systems 2018 mit einem zielgruppenorientierten Angebot als Partner für innovative Technologielösungen posi-tionieren. Ziel war es, Interaktionen zu schaffen und mit span-nenden Hands-On-Erlebnissen ein positives Image zu stärken.

The Tech Open Air (TOA) is Europe's largest interdisciplinary technology festival. The trendy event in Berlin attracts up to 15,000 visitors every year – the perfect place for a tech-nology company to get in touch with one's highly involved target group. T-Systems's goal in 2018 was to position itself there as a partner for innovative technology solutions with a target-group-orientated programme. The objective was to promote interaction and hands-on experiences that strengthened a positive brand image.

TARGET-GROUP-ORIENTATED HANDS-ON EXPERIENCES ARE DESIGNED TO PRO-MOTE INTERACTION AND STRENGTHEN IMAGE.

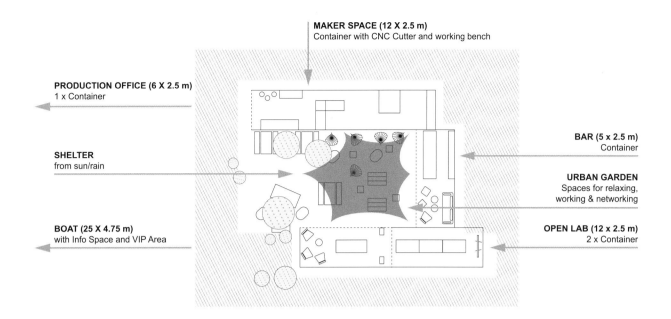

MAKER SPACE (12 X 2.5 m)
Container with CNC Cutter and working bench

PRODUCTION OFFICE (6 X 2.5 m)
1 x Container

SHELTER
from sun/rain

BOAT (25 X 4.75 m)
with Info Space and VIP Area

BAR (5 x 2.5 m)
Container

URBAN GARDEN
Spaces for relaxing,
working & networking

OPEN LAB (12 X 2.5 m)
2 x Container

PHOCUS BRAND CONTACT entwickelte dafür den Magenta Urban Garden, der auf der Außenfläche des alten Funkhauses seinen Platz fand. Die von Containern umrahmte Aktionsfläche bot den Festivalbesuchern einen Ort zum Entspannen, Lernen und Handwerken. Im Maker Space konnten Besucher ihren eigenen digitalen Stuhl designen und erhielten einen vor Ort mit einer CNC-Fräse produzierten Johan Stool als Dankeschön. Das Open Lab bot verschiedene Workshops zu Themen wie Blockchain und Distributed Ledger Technology. Die in der Mitte angesiedelte offene Fläche mit Bar diente als Ort zum Entspannen, Arbeiten und Netzwerken. Neben einem ganzheitlichen Vor-Ort-Kommunikationskonzept für die TOA wurde das Event von einer breit angelegten Social-Media-Kampagne auf XING, Facebook und Twitter begleitet.

PHOCUS BRAND CONTACT developed the Magenta Urban Garden in the outdoor space of the old Funkhaus with this goal in mind. Enclosed by containers, the event space offered the festival visitors a place to relax, learn, and create. In the Maker Space, visitors could design their own digital chairs, and received a Johan Stool (that was produced on site with a CNC lathe) as a thank you. The Open Lab hosted diverse workshops on topics like blockchain and distributed ledger technology. There was an open space with a bar in the middle for relaxing, working, and networking. In addition to the comprehensive communication concept on-site at TOA, the event was accompanied by a wide-sweeping social media campaign on XING, Facebook, and Twitter.

FRAUNHOFER ANNUAL CONVENTION 2019
ONLIVELINE GMBH – BÜRO FÜR KONZEPTION & INSZENIERUNG, COLOGNE

Location
Bolle Ballrooms, Berlin

Client
Fraunhofer-Gesellschaft zur Förderung der angewandten Forschung e.V., Munich

Month / Year
May 2018

Duration
2 days

Dramaturgy / Direction / Coordination
onliveline GmbH, Cologne

Media
Heinz Stricker media3 comunication, Essen;
Daniel Kaminski (pandoras box)

Music
Matz Flores & Qosono

Artists / Show acts
Sonja Kling (Explora)

Interactive Laser
Frieder Weiss

Decoration
satis&fy AG, Karben

Others
PRG Production Resource Group AG
(Technology)

Photos
onliveline GmbH, Cologne

Die Jahrestagung der Fraunhofer-Gesellschaft, einer der
größten deutschen Forschungsgesellschaften, beschäftigte
sich 2018 mit „kognitiven Systemen". Zu diesem Fachbereich
gehört auch das Thema künstliche Intelligenz, das in die
Abendveranstaltung und Inszenierung integriert werden
sollte. Das Konzept von onliveline sah eine spielerische
Visualisierung, die gleichzeitig hinterfragt und Diskussionen
anregt, vor. Diese Aufgabe sollte „Explora" erfüllen – eine
interaktive Personifizierung künstlicher Intelligenz.

DAS THEMA KI WIRD IN EINER INSZENIERTEN PERSONIFIZIERUNG NAMENS „EXPLORA" GREIFBAR GEMACHT.

The annual convention of the Fraunhofer society, one of
the largest German research societies, was involved with
"cognitive systems" in 2018. This specialist area also includes
the topic of artificial intelligence, which was to be integrated into the evening event and staging. The concept put
forward by onliveline envisaged a playful visualisation that
both questions and stimulates discussions. This task was
designed to realise "Explora" – an interactive personifica-
tion of artificial intelligence.

Eine transparente Nylonfadenskulptur, die sich im gesamten Gebäude wiederfand, diente als Projektionsfläche und ermöglichte „Explora", in Erscheinung zu treten. Als virtuelle Komoderatorin führte „Explora" durch den Abend, interagierte mit der Bühne und dem Publikum, präsentierte ihre Recherchen und Gedanken – und entwickelte sich im Verlauf des Events immer weiter. Szenen verdeutlichten ihr Lernvermögen, sie begann zu gestalten und Teile der Moderation zu übernehmen, um schließlich visionär mit den menschlichen Darstellern zusammenzuarbeiten. Projektionen, interaktive Laser, 3-D-Soundinstallationen und die Entwicklung einer visuellen Landschaft dienten als mediale Hilfsmittel, um „Explora" darzustellen und Visionen, Möglichkeiten und Ängste rund um künstliche Intelligenz dramaturgisch zu inszenieren.

THE TOPIC OF AI IS MADE TANGIBLE THROUGH A STAGE PERSONIFICATION CALLED "EXPLORA".

A transparent nylon thread sculpture throughout the building served as a projection surface and enabled "Explora" to appear. As a virtual co-presenter, "Explora" provided guidance through the evening, interacted with the stage and the public, presented her research and thoughts – and developed further over the course of the event. Scenes revealed her learning capacity as she began to design and take over parts of the presentation, before finally cooperating in a visionary manner with the human presenters. Projections, interactive lasers, 3D installations and the development of a visual landscape served as media support to present "Explora" and to set the stage dramaturgically for visions, possibilities and concerns surrounding artificial intelligence.

UN CLIMATE CHANGE CONFERENCE 2017 (COP23)
VAGEDES & SCHMID GMBH, MARCEL REMELSKY, HAMBURG

Location
WCCB Bonn & Recreational area Rheinaue (artificial temporary conference city), Bonn

Client
Federal Ministry of the Environment, Nature Conservation and Nuclear Safety – BMU, Berlin, Bonn

Month / Year
November 2017

Duration
several days

Awards
BOB Award 2018; German Design Award 2019; Gold at BrandEX Award 2019

Direction / Coordination / Architecture / Design
Vagedes & Schmid GmbH, Hamburg

Graphics
Dada Design, Bonn

Lighting
Neumann&Müller

Decoration
mac messe- und ausstellungscenter Service GmbH; Schnaitt Internationale Messe- und Ladenbau GmbH, Bergheim

Catering
Broich Premium Catering GmbH; Food affairs GmbH, Heidenheim an der Brenz

Realisation
Neptunus GmbH, Dusseldorf; RÖDER Zelt- und Veranstaltungsservice GmbH, Büdingen; Losberger GmbH, Bad Rappenau

Others
Party Rent Group; RAD Sicherheit GmbH & Co. KG, Cologne

Photos
Dominik Ketz Photography, Bad Neuenahr-Ahrweiler

Der 23. Weltklimagipfel (COP23) fand im November 2017 in Bonn statt. Die 12-tägige Veranstaltung war die größte zwischenstaatliche Konferenz, die es in Deutschland je gab. 26.000 Teilnehmer aus 196 Ländern und 7.000 Crewmitglieder aus 70 Gewerken mussten bedacht werden. Für die Brandschutz- und Sicherheitskonzepte sowie ein Hochwasserkonzept waren diverse Bonner Behörden eingebunden. Zudem sollte die Rheinaue, auf der temporäre Bauten platziert wurden, möglichst unbeschädigt bleiben. Hinzu kam, dass der Klimagipfel erstmals mit einem klimafreundlichen Veranstaltungsmanagement nach EMAS (Eco-Management and Audit Scheme) umgesetzt wurde. Das übergeordnete Ziel war es, die Umweltauswirkungen der COP23 nachweislich so gering wie möglich zu halten. Eine Vielzahl komplexer Faktoren, die Vagedes & Schmid in nur 9 Monaten koordinierte.

A COMPLEX LARGE-SCALE EVENT BECOMES A TEMPORARY CITY REALISED ACCORDING TO EMAS IN JUST NINE MONTHS.

The 23rd United Nations Climate Change Conference (COP23) was held in November 2017 in Bonn. The 12-day event was the largest international conference ever to take place in Germany. 26,000 participants from 196 countries and 7000 crew members from 70 sites had to be taken into consideration. Various Bonn authorities were brought in for the fire protection and safety concepts, as well as a flood concept. In addition, the Rheinaue area on which temporary buildings were placed should remain as undamaged as possible. Furthermore, the climate summit was realised for the first time with an environmentally friendly event management according to EMAS (Eco-Management and Audit Scheme). A superordinate aim was to keep the environmental impact of COP23 as verifiably minimal as possible. Vagedes & Schmid coordinated these many complex factors in just 9 months.

EIN KOMPLEXES GROSSEVENT WIRD IN NEUN MONATEN ZU EINER TEMPORÄREN NACH EMAS UMGESETZTEN KONFERENZSTADT.

Das Konzept bestand darin, einen kreativen Ort für Verhandlungen, persönlichen Austausch und Vernetzung der Teilnehmer zu gestalten. Es sollte eine „Blue Zone" als Verhandlungsbereich und eine „Green Zone" als messeähnliche Plattform entstehen. Da das Bonner World Conference Center und der UN-Campus hierfür nicht ausreichten, errichtete die Agentur eine ergänzende, zweigeteilte und 55.000 Quadratmeter große Stadt aus temporären Bauten. Die inhaltlichen Vorgaben wurden in einer „Bula Zone" (fidschianisch für „willkommen") umgesetzt, in der die offiziellen Klimaschutzverhandlungen stattfanden. Die „Bonn Zone" (bzw. „Green Zone") wurde in die Rheinaue, einen öffentlichen Park am Rhein, verlegt. Dort wurden in einer temporären Zeltstadt Lösungsansätze gezeigt und diskutiert. In Anlehnung an die COP-Präsidentschaft des Inselstaates Fidschi sollte die schlichte Gestaltung mit gezielten Kontrasten, großformatigen Bildern und fidschianischen Begrüßungen auf wellenförmigen Wandelementen ein „Fidschi-Look-and-Feel" erzeugen.

The concept consisted of designing a creative venue for events, personal exchanges and the networking of the participants. A "Blue Zone" was to be created as a negotiation area and a "Green Zone" as a platform similar to a trade fair. As the Bonn World Conference Centre and the UN Campus were not adequate for this, the agency built a supplementary two-part city of temporary buildings spanning 55,000 square metres. The content specifications were realised in a "Bula Zone" (Fijian for "welcome") in which the official climate protection negotiations took place. The "Bonn Zone" (or "Green Zone") was relocated to the Rheinaue area, a public park by the Rhine. Possible solutions were demonstrated and discussed there in a temporary tent city. In reference to the COP presidency of the island state of Fiji, the sleek design with targeted contrasts, large-format images and Fijian greetings on wave-shaped wall elements was intended to generate a "Fiji look and feel".

Im Gegensatz zu den regulären Kategorien setzt diese Sonderkategorie einen anderen Fokus. Anstatt Zielgruppen herauszustellen, stehen die Gestalter im Mittelpunkt: der Nachwuchs.

STUDENT PROJECTS: KATEGORIEÜBERGREIFENDE SEMESTERARBEITEN UND EVENTPROJEKTE, DIE VON STUDIERENDENTEAMS UNTERSCHIEDLICHER STUDIENRICHTUNGEN KONZIPIERT WURDEN. DEM KÖNNEN SOWOHL FIKTIVE FRAGESTELLUNGEN ALS AUCH ZIELVORGABEN VON ECHTEN AUFTRAGGEBERN ZUGRUNDE LIEGEN. DIE UMSETZUNG ERFOLGT TEILWEISE IN KOMPLETTER EIGENREGIE ODER MIT UNTERSTÜTZUNG VON ERFAHRENEN FACHLEUTEN.

Contrary to the regular categories, this special category sets a different focus.
Instead of focussing on target groups, the designers are at the centre: up-and-coming
designers.

STUDENT PROJECTS: STUDY PROJECTS AND EVENT PROJECTS CONCEIVED BY VARIOUS FIELDS OF STUDY ACROSS DIFFERENT CATEGORIES. THESE CAN BE BASED ON BOTH FICTIVE SUBJECT MATTERS AND SPECIFICATIONS BY REAL CLIENTS. THE REALISATION IS IN SOME CASES COMPLETELY INDEPENDENT OR ELSE WITH THE SUPPORT OF EXPERIENCED SPECIALISTS.

AUTO:PROTO:TYP
PFORZHEIM UNIVERSITY, SCHOOL OF DESIGN, DESIGN PF FAKULTÄT FÜR GESTALTUNG

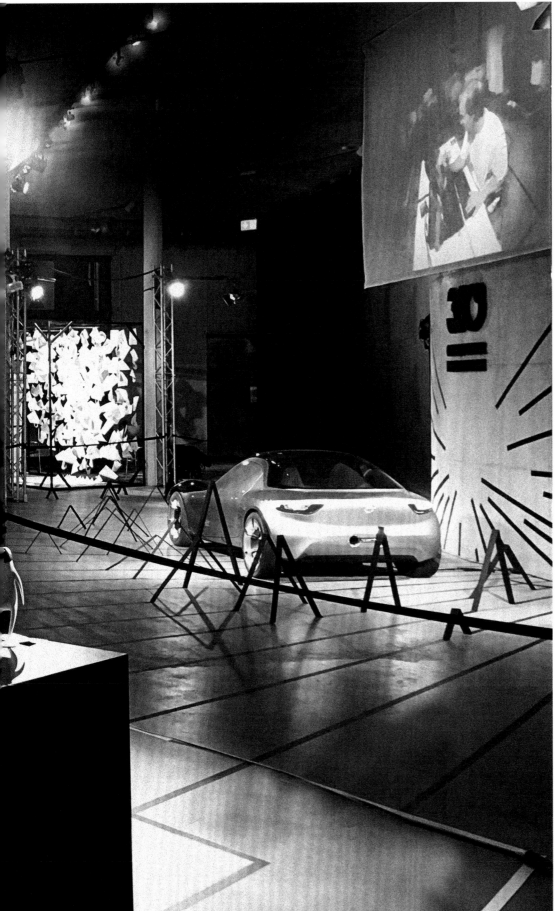

Location
Gasometer Pforzheim

Client
Pforzheim University, School of Design

Month / Year
July 2017

Duration
4 days

Dramaturgy
Steffen Vetterle

Direction / Coordination
Monika Markert, Achim Römer, Steffen Vetterle

Architecture / Design
Steffen Vetterle & Students: Ömer Gör, Selin Kaydok, Louis von Lohr, Rose Huyhn, Linda Schannen, Natalie Schnekenburger, Sarah Tribula

Graphics
Ömer Gör, Rose Huyhn, Linda Schannen

Lighting
Bernhard Gruber-Ballehr, Fichtner Tontechnik, Tübingen

Media
Julius Schuster (Voiceover / Speaker), Ömer Gör (GoPro Camera), Fabian Lörz (Sound)

Films
Michal Plata (GoPro Transmission on central projection surface, Film "Tape-Drawing")

Music
Fabian Lörz (Sound)

Artists / Show acts
Students of the Study programme Transportation Design

Realisation
Students of the Study programmes Transportation Design + Visual Communication

Photos
Harald Koch, Steffen Vetterle

Für das Ausstellungsprojekt „auto:proto:typ" arbeiteten die Studiengänge Transportation Design und Visuelle Kommunikation (Kommunikation im Raum) der Hochschule Pforzheim erstmals zusammen. Im Gasometer Pforzheim entwickelten sie eine theaterähnliche und unkonventionelle Präsentation des Konzeptfahrzeugs Concept GT von Opel. In Anlehnung an den Lars-von-Trier-Film *Dogville* skizzierte das Studierendenteam mithilfe von Tape Art fünf Räume. Sie sollten den chronologischen Werkprozess im Studium und der Industrie wiedergeben. Vom ersten Raum „Ideation/Zeichnen" über „Tape-Drawing", „CAD-Modelling" bis „Clay-Modelling" und schlussendlich im fünften Raum mit dem Ausarbeiten von maßstäblichen Modellen. Zentrales Verbindungsstück aller Räume war die Highlight Stage, auf der sich das verhüllte Konzeptfahrzeug befand.

For the exhibition project "auto:proto:typ", the study programmes Transportation Design and Visual Communication (Communication in Space) at Pforzheim University worked together for the first time. They developed a theatrical and unconventional presentation of the concept vehicle Concept GT by Opel at the Gasometer Pforzheim. In reference to the Lars von Trier film *Dogville*, the team of students sketched five rooms using tape art. They were designed to represent the chronological work process in studies and industry, from the first room "Ideation/drawing" to "tape drawing", "CAD modelling", "clay modelling" and finally the fifth room with the development of scale models. The central connecting element of all the rooms was the Highlight Stage, where the concealed concept car stood.

THEATERÄHNLICHE SZENEN ERKLÄREN DEN WERKPROZESS UND SCHAFFEN EINE UNKONVENTIONELLE AUTOPRÄSENTATION.

Durch die Vernissage mit 150 Gästen führte eine chronologische Dramaturgie. Während die Gäste sich frei im Raum bewegten, erlosch das Licht, ein eigens entwickelter Sound erklang und eine Stimme aus dem Off begann von der Ideenfindung zu erzählen. In diesem Moment wurde der erste Raum „Ideation /Zeichnen" mit Spotlights erhellt. Zwei Studenten betraten die Szenerie, setzten sich an den Schreibtisch und begannen zu zeichnen. In diesem theaterähnlichen Stil wurden auch die weiteren Räume und Themen erklärt. Live-Taping-Einlagen bildeten die Übergänge. Die Szenen wurden filmisch mit einer GoPro begleitet und direkt auf eine in der Mitte angebrachte Projektionsfläche übertragen. Zum Finale der 20-minütigen Performance wurde das bis dahin verhüllte Konzeptauto durch die Protagonisten der einzelnen Szenen enthüllt.

A chronological dramaturgy led through the vernissage with 150 guests. While the guests moved freely through the room, the light went out, a specially developed sound resounded and a voice from the off started recounting the idea generation. At that moment, the first room "Ideation / drawing" was illuminated with spotlights. Two students entered the scene, sat down at the desk and started drawing. The other rooms and themes were also explained in this theatrical style. Live taping inserts formed transitions. The scenes were accompanied cinematically by a GoPro and transmitted directly to a projection surface mounted in the middle. For the finale of the 20-minute performance, the hitherto concealed concept car was uncovered by the protagonists in the individual scenes.

THEATRICAL SCENES EXPLAIN THE WORK PROCESS AND CREATE AN UNCONVENTIONAL CAR PRESENTATION.

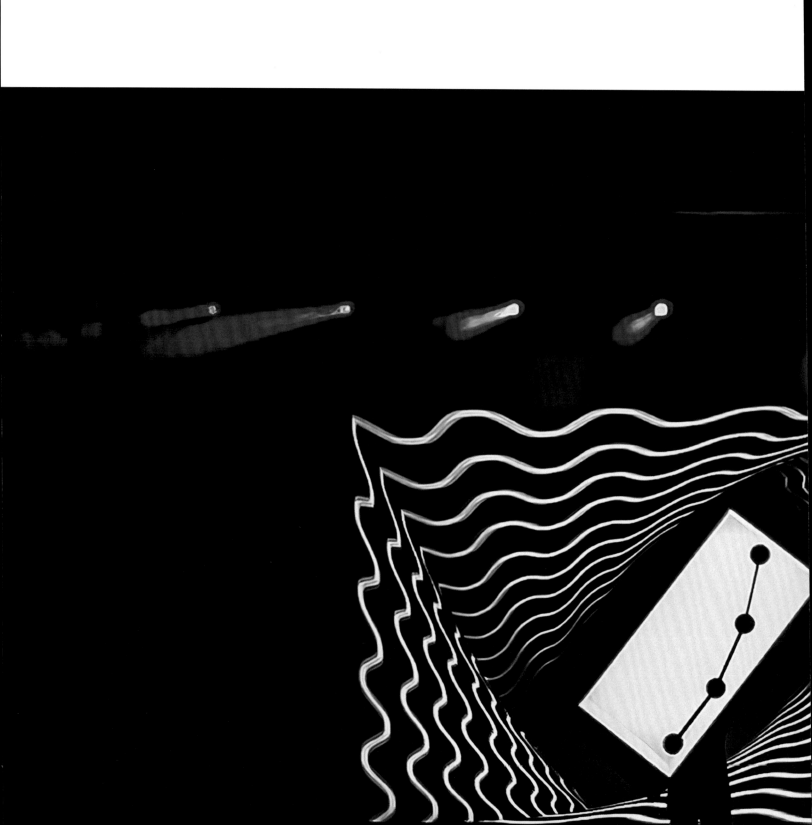

PROJECT:ON – STAGE SHOW OF THE FUTURE
UNIVERSITY OF APPLIED SCIENCES KAISERSLAUTERN, VIRTUAL DESIGN

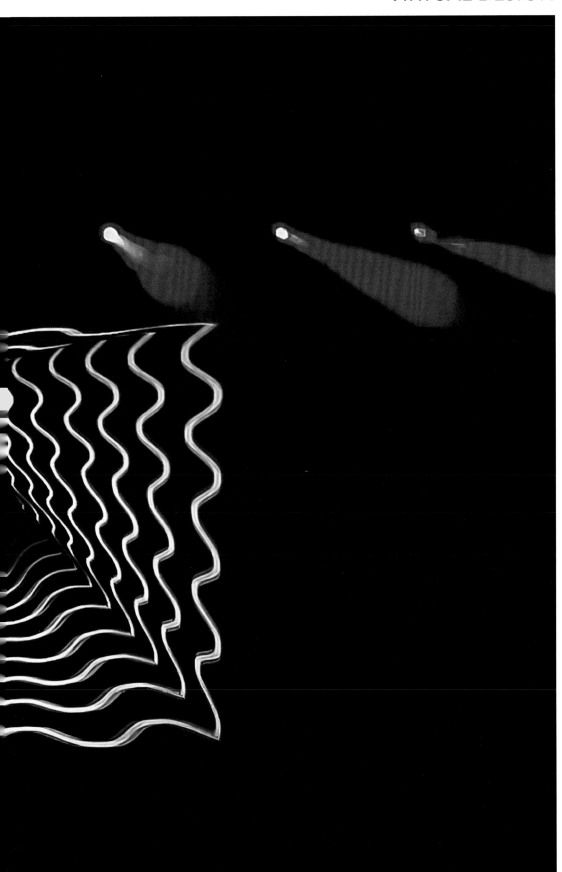

Location
Kammgarn Kaiserslautern

Client
Startup Westpfalz e.V.

Month / Year
August 2017

Duration
1 day

Awards
Goldener Nagel at ADC Juniorwettbewerb 2018, Bronze at CommAward 2018

Creators
Niklas Blume, Philip Greiner-Petter, Melina Kaiser, Lisa Lauer, Manuel Peris, Dimitri Saenko, Caroline Seibert, Alina Wingert

Supervisors
Prof. Matthias Pfaff,
Prof. Christian Schmachtenberg

Lighting
Kammgarn Kaiserslautern

Artists / Show acts
Meik Landfried (Actor)

Photos
Christian Schmachtenberg, Melina Kaiser, Manuel Peris

Internet
https://youtu.be/2NlzvL47ELQ
https://youtu.be/KgqaMVIoHM8

For a semester paper in the year 2017, a team of students at University of Applied Sciences Kaiserslautern developed a project called "Project:on – Stage Show of the Future". The task was to open a start-up event with an innovative stage show. In terms of content, the key theme of "Transformation" was to be presented in a contemporary manner worthy of the start-up idea. The stage of a concert house with around 1000 seats served as the venue for the realisation.

EINE ECHTZEIT-INTERAKTION ZWISCHEN SCHAUSPIELER UND PROJEKTION ALS INNOVATIVE BÜHNENSHOW.

A REAL-TIME INTERACTION BETWEEN AN ACTOR AND PROJECTION AS AN INNOVATIVE STAGE SHOW.

Für eine Semesterarbeit im Jahr 2017 entwickelte ein Studierendenteam der Hochschule Kaiserslautern ein Projekt namens „Project:on – Bühnenshow der Zukunft". Die Aufgabe bestand darin, eine Startup-Veranstaltung mit einer innovativen Bühnenshow zu eröffnen. Inhaltlich sollte das Leitthema „Transformation" in zeitgemäßer und dem Startup-Gedanken würdiger Art und Weise umgesetzt werden. Die Bühne eines Konzerthauses mit etwa 1.000 Sitzplätzen diente als Umsetzungsort.

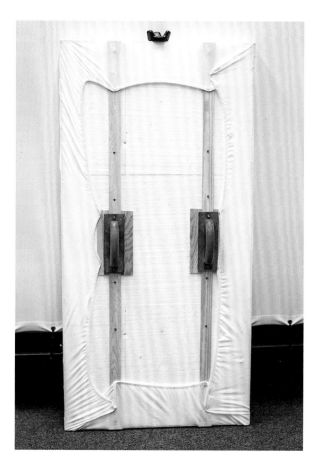

The students decided on a projection mapping that, together with an actor, recounted an abstract metamorphosis from a caterpillar to a butterfly. Apart from a large rear projection screen, a small mobile screen served as a complementary surface for the projected content. The special feature: the actor could actually interact with the mobile screen in real time and thereby influence the projection and the overall result. This project was realised with the tracking technology of the virtual reality glasses HTC Vive. This allowed the screen, fitted with a tracker, to be followed in the room and be incorporated into the projection as an object. A contemporary and sophisticated work both technically and in terms of design that can easily hold its own with any event planned by an agency!

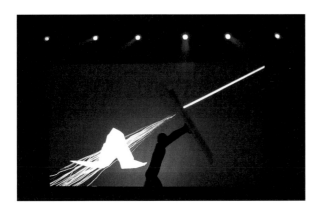

Die Studierenden entschieden sich für ein Projection Mapping, das gemeinsam mit einem Schauspieler über eine abstrakte Metamorphose von einer Raupe zu einem Schmetterling erzählte. Neben einer großen Rückprojektionsleinwand diente eine kleine, mobile Leinwand als ergänzende Fläche für die projizierten Inhalte. Die Besonderheit: Der Schauspieler konnte mit der mobilen Leinwand in Echtzeit tatsächlich interagieren und so Einfluss auf die Projektion sowie das Gesamtergebnis nehmen. Realisiert wurde dieses Projekt mit der Tracking-Technologie der VR-Brille HTC Vive. Darüber konnte die Leinwand, mit einem Tracker ausgestattet, im Raum verfolgt und als Objekt in die Projektion einbezogen werden. Eine technisch wie gestalterisch zeitgemäße und anspruchsvolle Arbeit, die es mit jedem von einer Agentur geplanten Event locker aufnehmen kann!

INFLUENZA–M. MODE STECKT AN
PFORZHEIM UNIVERSITY, SCHOOL OF DESIGN, DESIGN PF FAKULTÄT FÜR GESTALTUNG

Location
Alfons Kern Tower, City area and River Enz, Pforzheim

Client
Cultural Department of Pforzheim / EMMA-Kreativzentrum

Month / Year
October – December 2018

Duration
6 weeks

Dramaturgy
Sarah Tribula, Steffen Vetterle & Fashion students

Direction / Coordination
Steffen Vetterle, Prof. Johann Stockhammer

Architecture / Design
Sarah Tribula, Rose Huyhn, Linda Schannen, Saskia Lorenz, Alexander Diez, Laura Ragusa

Graphics
Saskia Lorenz, Sarah Tribula, Jan Hubl

Lighting
belzner holmes, Stuttgart; Vecordia, Calw

Media
Jan Hubl a.k.a. zwischendrunter (Façade mapping); Daniel Steinfels a.k.a. tonal (Sound)

Films / Animation
20 Films by Fashion students

Music
Daniel Steinfels a.k.a. tonal (Sound)

Artists / Show acts
Ballett Theater Pforzheim, Students, Kultur Schaffer e.V.

Catering
Café Roland

Realisation
Alfons Kern School (Exhibition furniture)

Photos
Janusz Czech, Harald Koch, Steffen Vetterle

Fashion is an enormously important aspect of our society across all generations. What is changing are not only the designs but also the way we consume and view fashion. How could new, communicative, dramaturgic and spatially tangible formats of "fashion show(ing)" present themselves? This question was put to a team of students of the Fashion and Visual Communication (Communication in Space) Programme at Pforzheim University. Their result was a multifaceted 6-week event under the name "Influenza–M".

The prelude was formed by a vernissage that opened the central exhibition at the Alfons Kern Tower. After concluding the official part, the guests were released directly onto a white catwalk in the outdoor area. This was a change of perspective that was reinforced by 100 models and extras next to the catwalk and marked the beginning of various events.

Mode ist ein über alle Generationen hinweg enorm wichtiger Aspekt unserer Gesellschaft. Es ändern sich nicht nur die Designs, sondern auch die Art und Weise, wie wir Mode konsumieren und schauen. Wie könnten also neue, kommunikative, dramaturgisch und räumlich erlebbare Formate des „Mode Schau(ens)" aussehen? Dieser Frage ging ein Studierendenteam der Studiengänge Mode und Visuelle Kommunikation (Kommunikation im Raum) der Hochschule Pforzheim nach. Ihr Ergebnis war eine vielseitige, 6-wöchige Veranstaltung unter dem Namen „Influenza–M".

EINE MODENSCHAU ALS ÖFFENTLICHES ERLEBNIS – MIT PERFORMANCES AN BUSHALTESTELLEN UND IM BUS.

Den Auftakt bildete eine Vernissage, die die zentrale Ausstellung im Alfons-Kern-Turm eröffnete. Nach Abschluss des offiziellen Teils wurden die Gäste unvermittelt auf einen weißen Catwalk im Außenbereich entlassen. Ein Perspektivwechsel, der durch 100 Models und Statisten neben dem Catwalk verstärkt wurde und den Anfang verschiedenster Aktionen markierte.

Illuminierte Zorbbälle und Hunderte Blitzlichter inszenierten auf der durch Pforzheim fließenden Enz den Ausbruch der Influenza–M. Ein Projection Mapping hüllte den Alfons-Kern-Turm in textile und abstrakte Muster, spielte mit vergangenen Modepräsentationen und dem Thema Virusausbruch. Tänzerinnen und Tänzer des Ballett Theater Pforzheim untermalten die Raumbilder der Ausstellung im Inneren des Turms. Die dazugehörige Modenschau fand 2018 im öffentlichen Raum statt – unter anderem in der Influenza–M Fashion Line, einer Buslinie mit eigenem Verkehrsnetz. Kollektionen wurden im Bus oder an Haltestellen performt, konzeptionell miteinander verknüpft und von eingeweihten Besuchern und Passanten begleitet. Mode-Workshops, Vorträge und ein Kinoprogramm ergänzten das veranstaltungsreiche Konzept.

A FASHION SHOW AS A PUBLIC EXPERIENCE – WITH PERFORMANCES AT BUS STOPS AND IN THE BUS.

Illuminated zorb balls and hundreds of flashing lights staged the outbreak of Influenza–M on the Enz flowing through Pforzheim. A projection mapping cloaked the Alfons Kern Tower in textile and abstract patterns, played with past fashion presentations and the topic of a viral outbreak. Dancers from the Ballet Theater Pforzheim accompanied the spatial design of the exhibition inside the tower. The associated fashion show was held in the public space in 2018 – including in the Influenza–M fashion line, a bus line with its own transport network. Collections were performed in the bus or at stops, linked conceptually and accompanied by initiated visitors and passers-by. Fashion workshops, presentations and a cinema programme rounded off the event-packed concept.

HANDWERKER GAMES
PROF. STEFAN LUPPOLD: DHBW RAVENSBURG

Location
Oberschwabenhalle, Ravensburg

Client
Kreishandwerkerschaft Ravensburg

Month / Year
November 2018

Duration
2 days

Photos
A. & T. Schmid GbR Messe-Süd

EIN SPIELERISCHER UND EMOTIONALER WETTBEWERB SOLL FÜR HAND-WERKLICHE BERUFE BEGEISTERN.

Bei 37.000 Ausbildungsplätzen, die deutschlandweit unbesetzt bleiben, sorgt sich das Handwerk um sein Image – vor allem bei Jugendlichen. Eine klassische Informationsveranstaltung ist jedoch kaum die Lösung, um Begeisterung für handwerkliche Berufe zu schüren. Dessen war sich auch die Kreishandwerkerschaft Ravensburg bewusst und tat sich mit Studierenden des Studiengangs Messe-, Kongress- und Eventmanagement der DHBW Ravensburg zusammen. Ein sechsköpfiges Studierendenteam entwickelte ein Konzept, das mit spielerischen und emotional aufgeladenen Elementen gezielt Jugendliche ansprechen und gleichzeitig auch Eltern und Lehrer einbinden sollte: die Handwerker Games.

With 37,000 trainee places vacant Germany-wide, the vocational trades are concerned about their image – especially among young people. However, a traditional information event is scarcely the solution for sparking enthusiasm for vocational professions. The District Trades Association (KHW) Ravensburg was also aware of this and got together with students of the Trade Fair, Congress and Event Management course at DHBW Ravensburg. A team of six students developed a concept designed to appeal in a targeted manner to young people with playful and emotionally charged elements, whilst also incorporating parents and teachers: the Trade Games.

A PLAYFUL AND EMOTIONAL COMPETITION IS DESIGNED TO INSPIRE ENTHUSIASM FOR VOCATIONAL TRADES.

In Anlehnung an die „Hunger Games" aus der Film- und Romanreihe *Die Tribute von Panem* durchliefen Schülerteams der 8. Klasse verschiedene Stationen, an denen sie gegeneinander antreten mussten. Die jeweils zu bewältigenden Aufgaben repräsentierten die verschiedenen Innungen. Beispielsweise stellte die Elektro-Innung Ravensburg das E-Handwerk im Bereich eines Segway-Parcours vor. Ein Speed Dating mit Azubis sowie eine Ausstellung mit Ständen der Innungen boten zusätzliche Informationsmöglichkeiten für Schüler und Eltern. Daneben beinhaltete die zweitägige Veranstaltung eine Moderation, Show-Acts und Catering. So kämpften bei der Premiere mehrere Hundert Schüler um Pokale und Geldpreise für die Klassenkasse. Eine Fortsetzung der Handwerker Games ist bereits geplant.

In reference to the "Hunger Games" from the eponymous film and fiction series, teams of 8th grade pupils passed through various stations where they had to compete against each other. The tasks to be mastered represented the various guilds. For example, the Ravensburg electricity guild presented the trade in the area of a Segway course. Speed dating with apprentices as well as an exhibition with guild stands offered additional information options for pupils and parents. Alongside this, the two-day event included a presentation, show acts and catering. At the premiere, several hundred pupils thus competed for trophies and money prizes for the class fund. A sequel to the Trade Games is already planned.

Jan Kalbfleisch, gute Live-Kommunikation sollte eigentlich schon immer die Besucher in den Fokus stellen. Trotzdem scheinen die Gäste und ihre Interessen heute eine größere Bedeutung zu haben. Hat sich tatsächlich etwas geändert?

Nicht nur beim Angeln, sondern auch in allen Disziplinen der Kommunikation gilt ja von jeher, dass der Wurm dem Fisch schmecken muss und nicht dem Angler. Allerdings ist in unserem Beispiel der Angler schon auch immer in latenter Gefahr, dem Fisch erklären zu wollen, dass ihm der dargebotene Wurm schon zu schmecken hat.

Doch die Auswahl an Würmern hat zugenommen. Live-Kommunikation ist in ihrer Bedeutung als strategisches Kommunikationsinstrument deutlich gestiegen. Immer mehr Unternehmen erkennen die Vorteile unserer Kommunikationsgattung und setzen diese vermehrt ein. Für uns als Branche ist diese Entwicklung – wenn sie auch noch lange nicht am Ziel ist – rundweg positiv und das Ergebnis langer und anstrengender Kommunikation mit den Kunden. Es führt jedoch auch dazu, dass der Wettbewerb unter den unterschiedlichen Formaten und Möglichkeiten zugenommen hat.

TEILNEHMER WÄHLEN SEHR GENAU AUS, WELCHEN VERAN-STALTUNGEN SIE IHRE BEGRENZTE AUFMERKSAMKEIT SCHENKEN.

Und da werden Formate, die der potenzielle Teilnehmer als für sich Nutzen stiftend erkennt, natürlich priorisiert. Die Kunden unserer Branche sind also gut beraten, nicht nur in Live-Kommunikation zu denken, sondern nach „Custom made"-Lösungen für sich und vor allem ihre Teilnehmer zu streben.

Haben sich konzeptionelle Vorgehensweisen in diesem Kontext verändert? Wird tatsächlich für jedes Event mehr analysiert, was sich die Besucher wünschen?

Big Data in der Live-Kommunikation? Fakt ist, es wird heute deutlich mehr gemessen, erhoben und analysiert als vor wenigen Jahren. Dabei ist wohl aber weniger das Streben nach einer optimierten Konzeption der Treiber als die immerwährende Controlling-Frage nach Output im Verhältnis zum Input. Die alte Formel „Wir haben viel Kaffee ausgeschenkt – also war viel los bei uns", ist wohl endgültig obsolet.

Stattdessen werden Handys angetriggert, User identifiziert, angereichert und profiliert. Heatmaps zeigen den genauen Traffic einer Veranstaltung zu jeder Sekunde der Laufzeit. Optische Systeme erkennen Standbesucher und verfolgen deren Interessen und Verweilzeiten. All die gesammelten Daten werden zurückgespielt in die CRM des Veranstalters. Natürlich alles streng nach DSGVO. Und dann? Nun, bei weitgehend eindeutiger Datenlage werden sicher die richtigen Schlüsse gezogen und Maßnahmen eingeleitet. Es ist jedoch eher anzuzweifeln, dass die generierten Daten auf breiter Front eine so eindeutige und wirklich verwertbare Datenbasis darstellen.

Auch die bekannten Giganten der Datensammlung und -analyse liefern bis heute oftmals eher zweifelhaften Output. Wer als 30-Jähriger schon mal auf Facebook mit Werbung für Treppenlifte überrascht wurde, weiß, was gemeint ist. Es ist anzuzweifeln, dass die auf diesem Wege gesammelten Daten tatsächlich von ausreichender Härte und Aussagekraft sind, als dass diese direkten und umfassenden Einfluss auf die Konzeption haben würden. Im Übrigen sind alle gesammelten Daten stets historisch. Und wir wissen aus vielen Bereichen des Lebens, dass nichts so alt ist wie die Erkenntnisse von gestern. Daher ist und bleibt handwerkliches Geschick, Erfahrung, Kreativität und Mut auch weiterhin der größere Teil erfolgreicher Live-Kommunikation.

Jan Kalbfleisch studierte Wirtschaftsingenieurwesen und ist Geschäftsführer des Fachverbands der Event- und Messebranche FAMAB Kommunikationsverband e.V.

www.famab.de

VON ANGLERN UND WÜRMERN
OF FISHERMEN AND WORMS
COMMENTARY BY JAN KALBFLEISCH, FAMAB E. V.

Jan Kalbfleisch, good live communication was actually always supposed to place a focus on the visitors. Even so, the guests and their interests seem to have a greater significance today. Has anything in fact changed?

Not only when fishing, but also in all disciplines of communication it has always applied that the fish and not the fisherman must like the taste of the worm. However, in our example the fisherman is always in the latent danger of wanting to explain to the fish that it is supposed to like the proffered worm.

However, the choice of worms has increased. Live communication has significantly increased in importance as a strategic communication tool. More and more companies are recognising the advantages of our communication genre and are using it increasingly. For us as a sector, this development – even if it is still far from its goal – is altogether positive and the result of long and tiring communication with the customer. However, it also leads to competition among the different formats and possibilities increasing.

PARTICIPANTS CHOOSE VERY CAREFULLY WHAT EVENTS TO DEDICATE THEIR LIMITED ATTENTION TO.

And, of course, formats that the potential participant identifies as having a use for themselves are prioritized. The customers in our sector are therefore well-advised to not only think in terms of live communication but to strive for "custom-made" solutions for themselves and especially their participants.

Have conceptual approaches changed in this context? Is there indeed more analysis for each event of what the visitors wish for?

Big Data in live communication? The fact is, today there is significantly more measuring, gathering and analysing than just a few years ago. However, it is no doubt less about the striving for an optimised concept by the operators than the constant controlling question about output in relation to input. The old formula "We have poured a lot of coffee – so there was a lot happening" is undoubtedly definitively obsolete.

Instead, mobiles are triggered, users are identified, substantiated and profiled. Heat maps show the exact traffic of an event at every second of its duration. Optical systems identify stand visitors and follow their interests and visiting times. All the gathered data is fed back into the CRM of the organiser. Of course, all strictly according to the GDPR. And then? Well, if there is largely conclusive data then no doubt the right conclusions are drawn and measures are introduced. However, it is rather doubtful whether the generated data represent such a clear and truly applicable data basis on a wide front.

Even the well-known giants of data gathering and analysis often supply rather doubtful output up until today. Those who were surprised on Facebook as a 30-year-old with advertising for stair lifts know what is meant by this. It is to be doubted that the data gathered in this manner is indeed sufficiently solid and revealing to have direct and comprehensive influence on conceptualising. In addition, all gathered data is already historical. And we know from many spheres of life that nothing is as old as yesterday's insights. Creative skill, experience, creativity and courage therefore are and remain the more major aspects of live communication.

Jan Kalbfleisch studied industrial engineering and is Managing Director of the Trade Association of the Event and Exhibition Industry FAMAB Kommunikationsverband e. V.

www.famab.de

∧ventem
Audiovisuelle Dienstleistungen

Service

Aventem offers high-level technical and constructional planning and implementation of corporate events, fair stands, television shows, and conferences.

In detail we offer media technics and services, illumination, audio, booth construction, rigging incl. SIL3 systems, stage and scenery.

Aventem provides full service, and delivers from its office and warehouse close to Dusseldorf to customers worldwide. With its own wood, electronic, and metal factory, as well as large logistc capacities Aventem offers great flexibility for the realisation of projects.

References

Deutsche Bank AG, Targo Bank, Deutsche Apotheker & Ärzte Bank, Verein Deutscher Ingenieure, MVDA / Linda AG, Allianz AG, ThyssenKrupp AG, Rittal GmbH & Co. KG, Vorwerk Elektrowerke GmbH & Co. KG, Rewe Zentral AG, Bayer AG, Siemens AG, E.ON, Uniper SE, RWE AG, Toyota Deutschland, Honda, Škoda AG, Volkswagen AG, Daimler AG, Falken Tyre Europe GmbH, MAN AG, Rheinmetall AG, Vodafone AG, Huawei Deutschland GmbH, Max Brinkmann KG, Zweites Deutsches Fernsehen, Westdeutscher Rundfunk, SWR, ARD

Contacts

Herderstraße 70
40721 Hilden
Germany
Phone: +49 2103 25230-0

Rohrdamm 24b
13629 Berlin
Germany
Phone: +49 30 367005-70

www.aventem.de
info@aventem.de

IMPRESSUM
IMPRINT

Author	Katharina Stein
Editing / Setting	Mario Ableitner
Translation	Lynne Kolar-Thompson
Layout	Tina Agard Grafik & Buchdesign, Esslingen / Neckar
Lithography	corinna rieber prepress, Marbach / Neckar
Printing	DZS GRAFIK, Ljubljana, Slovenia
Paper	GalerieArt Volume / 150 g/m²
Cover photo	raumkontakt GmbH, Karlsruhe

avedition GmbH
Publishers for Architecture and Design
Senefelderstr. 109
70176 Stuttgart
Germany
Tel.: +49 (0)711 / 220 22 79-0
Fax: +49 (0)711 / 220 22 79-15
eventdesign@avedition.de
www.avedition.com

ISBN 978-3-89986-312-3